Few realize that in the vast literature on prayer we find next to nothing written on prayer in the local church. I am thankful that Leon Franck is one who not only realizes it but is determined to do something about it. *Fresh Oil From Heaven—Helping [the] Church Become a House of Prayer* is a book that should be put into the hands of every pastor in America who desires new spiritual life and power to pour into the local church. (Quoted in 1992, first edition.)

—C. PETER WAGNER
FORMER PROFESSOR, FULLER THEOLOGICAL SEMINARY, PASADENA, CA

I love Pastor Leon Franck's book on prayer. It is a very practical guide of instructions on how to make your church a house of prayer. I am going to begin teaching at our church from this prayer manual. I am so excited to put these principals into action. After all, it was Jesus that called His house a "House of Prayer". I want to follow His example and become a house of prayer myself and follow through with making our church into a house of prayer.

—DIANE BLANCO
PASTOR OF PRAYER, RESURRECTION FELLOWSHIP, LOVELAND, CO

Pastor Franck captures the Holy Spirit's call to come back to "My house shall be called a house of prayer." Pastor Franck gives clear instruction and insight from a father's heart on how to get "family life" back into the church. I was able to use this book as my #1 textbook as I taught prayer leadership to hundreds of students at Christ for the Nations Institute. There was a tremendous response to this book from students from all over the world. I give it my highest recommendation.

—SALLY GREEN
FORMER DIRECTOR: HOUSE OF PRAYER
CHRIST FOR THE NATIONS INSTITUTE, DALLAS, TX

This book is a work of inspiration, worthwhile and timely. The author blends instruction and encouragement with motivation in a very readable way. Many parts are really excellent with genuine revelation teaching, especially "Secrets to Perseverance."

—DOROTHY MOORE
CHRISTIAN PSYCHOLOGIST & BIBLE TEACHER, PHOENIX, AZ

A profound and moving "life message" by a pastor who deeply loves the Church. Rev. Leon Franck's insights and teachings were forged, tested and proven on the anvil of real-life experience. As you reflect upon principles outlined in the end-of-chapter studies, you will be encouraged, refreshed and a⌐ ˙ ˙ ˙ ˙ʳ ˙ ˙ ˙ ˙ˡly releases an impartation - "oil from heaven."

PRESIDENT EM

T0170052

L
A

Having had the joy of visiting and praying with Leon Franck on various occasions, I have sensed his incredibly deep passion for prayer. Above all, his desire is that believers everywhere become people of prayer resulting in God's house truly being a house of prayer. Filled with practical insights, perspectives, and illustrations gleaned from many years of prayer ministry, *Fresh Oil from Heaven* is a must-read for pastors, prayer coordinators, and laity alike.

—JOHN T. MAEMPA
DIRECTOR, ASSEMBLIES OF GOD NATIONAL PRAYER CENTER

This is the most practical book on praying together that I have ever read.

—REV. ROBERT F. HOUSKA
PREVIOUS PASTOR, BETHEL FULL GOSPEL CHURCH
JOHNSTOWN, PA

This book lays the sequential, foundational, progression of prayer being the primary catalyst for the Word of God. It contains so many practical applications for success—full corporate intercession. A must read!

—REV. MARK SEPPO
PRAYER FACILITATOR FOR EASTERN MICHIGAN
ASSOC. PASTOR MARYSVILLE ASSEMBLY OF GOD
MARYSVILLE, MICHIGAN

Jesus said, "Could you not tarry one hour?" to His disciples. He told them also "When you pray...". Brother Leon has lived and shown through the Scriptures the blessings of having a regular vibrant prayer life. Let the words of life of this man push you past your flesh into the realm of God's Holy Spirit. Leon is a man who has lived to see that prayer works and can make a profound difference in your life. Be open to God's Spirit speaking to you and watch and see how you are radically transformed through the power of prayer!

—PASTOR TIM MARTIN
NEW LIFE CHRISTIAN CHURCH
ATTICA, MICHIGAN

Leon Franck wants you and the Body of Christ to join together in a *Fresh Oil from Heaven* prayer movement. This book is written for you, your family and friends to be the Church that Jesus called a House of Prayer.

—BRENT WELCH, CFP, ChFC, CLU
MANAGING MEMBER
WELSHIRE CAPITAL, LLC

FRESH OIL

from

HEAVEN

HELPING THE CHURCH
BECOME A HOUSE
OF **PRAYER**

FRESH OIL
from
HEAVEN

HELPING THE CHURCH
BECOME A HOUSE
OF **PRAYER**

LEON FRANCK

HIGHERLIFE
DEVELOPMENT SERVICES, INC
Oviedo, Florida

Fresh Oil from Heaven—Helping the Church Become a House of Prayer
by Reverend Leon Franck

Published by HigherLife Development Services, Inc.
400 Fontana Circle
Building 1 – Suite 105
Oviedo, Florida 32765
(407) 563-4806
www.ahigherlife.com

Copyright © 2010 by Reverend Leon Franck

All rights reserved

ISBN 13: 978-1-935245-30-8
ISBN 10: 1-935245-30-9

Cover Design: Judith McKittrick Wright

Second Edition

10 11 12 13 — 9 8 7 6 5 4 3 2 1

Printed in the United States of America

DEDICATION

*This book is dedicated first to the Body of Christ whom I love
and for whom I pray. Secondly, I would like to dedicate this
book to my dear wife, Arlene, who has stood with me through
many ordeals to encourage and help me and also to my family
of five children who pray for us.*

TABLE OF CONTENTS

"It is written," he said to them,
"'My house will be called a house
of prayer,' but you are making it a
'den of robbers.'"

—Matthew 21:13 NIV

"I shall be anointed with fresh oil"

—Psalm 92:10b

Is this verse true of the church today and, if so, how?

THE CALL TO BE A HOUSE OF PRAYER

Is GOD CALLING you to pray? Is He calling you to lead prayer gatherings? Communicating with God one on one or with a group of people should be exciting, exhilarating, and educational in the kingdom of God!

Why is prayer so important?

Prayer is the key to joy in the Christian life.

Prayer carries the oil from heaven to make all things in the church run smoothly.

Prayer guards God's glory, for only certain aspects of God's glory are unleashed through answers to prayer.

Prayer is the womb out of which the life and power of the Spirit are birthed.

In Jesus's time, the religious centers seemed more interested in raising finances than in functioning as places of true worship. Jesus entered the temple of His day and radically declared, "It is written," he said to them, "'My house will be called a house of prayer,' but you are making it a 'den of robbers'" (Matt. 21:13 NIV).

Dear Christian leader, whether you are hosting a Bible study in your home or leading a congregation of thousands, I would like to take you on an exciting journey—the adventure of learning to build the house that Jesus wants—the house of prayer. Walk with me now, and I'll introduce you to what I've found to be the challenge and thrill of my lifetime!

Chapter 1

THE CHALLENGE OF A LIFETIME

DID YOU EVER see a picture of an angry Jesus? I believe I did once. Jesus had a whip over His head, and He was driving out the merchandisers from the temple. He was angry, and the caption of course reads, "My house shall be called a house of prayer." What a challenge!

Do you know that in the Old Testament the temple was not called a house of prayer? However, the prophet Isaiah saw that it would come in the future:

Even them I will bring to My holy mountain,
And make them joyful in My house of prayer.
Their burnt offerings and their sacrifices
Will be accepted on My altar;
For My house shall be called a house of prayer for all nations.
(Isa. 56:7)[1]

This is a prophecy fulfilled in the New Testament by the Lord Jesus Christ in the first year of His public ministry. Jesus was angry because the Jews were not placing a priority on prayer.

Now the Passover of the Jews was at hand, and Jesus went up to Jerusalem. And He found in the temple those who sold oxen and sheep and doves, and the moneychangers doing business. When He had made a whip of cords, He drove them all out of the temple, with the sheep and the oxen, and poured out the changers' money and overturned the tables. And He said to those who sold doves, "Take these things away! Do not make My Father's house a house of merchandise!" Then His disciples remembered that it was written, "Zeal for Your house has eaten Me up" (John 2:13-17).

3

The New Living Bible translates this last phrase, *"passion for God's house will consume me."* So, we see that Jesus was very upset that the temple was not being characterized as a house of prayer.

Matthew tells us that Jesus again went into the temple two years later.

> Jesus entered the temple area and drove out all who were buying and selling there. He overturned the tables of the money changers and the benches of those selling doves. "It is written," he said to them, "'My house will be called a house of prayer,' but you are making it a 'den of robbers'" (Matt. 21:12-13 NIV).

The zeal of Jesus Christ for prayer was so evident and so important that Mark and Dr. Luke recorded it as well in Luke 19:45-46 and Mark 11:17 ('den of robbers').

In fact, I want to share something that a lot of people don't realize. The account of the cleansing of the temple in Luke 19:41 is actually the second time Jesus cleansed the temple. Luke is the only one who recorded it. Luke said, "And when he was come near, he beheld the city, and he wept over it" (KJV). That word *weep* means a loud gushing cry. Jesus was not just angry in this account, He was broken-hearted. After He wept loud and bitter tears, He went into the city and turned over tables and chased people out of the temple who were there just to make money.

Make God's House "A House of Prayer!"

Jesus never characterized His house by anything but prayer. He didn't say it would be a house of preaching the Word, nor did He say it would be a house of musical concerts. In His zeal for the honor of God and the worship of God, He said that it shall be called a house of prayer.

Prayer is the crown of glory upon the house of God. Are we not robbing God of His glory when we do not pray? Isn't He robbed when we no longer permit Him to exercise His authority, will, and power in our midst through our prayers? We need to schedule more prayers gatherings in the church. I believe that Christians will be eager to pray once they see two things:

First, they must see the leadership in their church get excited about prayer.

Second, Christians will be enthusiastic to pray when they see more answers to their prayers and see themselves being used by God to change lives and history.

It is exciting to push back the gates of hell! Believers cannot help but be excited and exhilarated as they allow the supernatural to become the natural occurrence in their daily lives. If we're not praying, we're just kicking up religious dust—religious activity. The conquest may not be easy, but it will be glorious.

The challenge of a lifetime is to ask ourselves, "Is the temple of the Lord a house of prayer? If not, how can we make it such?"

Let's take a look at those words *temple* and *house*. Scripture shows us that the temple is the individual Christian.

> Or do you not know that your body is the temple of the Holy Spirit who is in you, whom you have from God, and you are not your own? For you were bought at a price. (1 Cor. 6:19-20a)

So, the temple of God is first of all the individual Christian's life. What happens when more than one Christian is in one room?

> For where two or three are gathered together in My name, I am there in the midst of them. (Matt. 18:20)

Given the size of this small group of two or three, I would like to suggest that the home is the second key aspect of the temple of God, the Church of God. Husband, wife, and children—the family, the household—must be a house of prayer.

The third key aspect of the temple of God is His Church where His people gather together to worship. Here the challenge to us is: Do people see my life as being one devoted to communion with God, one of prayer, one of walking with God so that I can be changed into His image?

No prayer and communion with God means no transformation into Christ's likeness.

Do my children see me kneeling and praying at home? Do they know that I esteem worship and prayer as the highest aspect of my life? Does my wife see me as a man who leads our home in prayer? Does my husband see me kneeling and praying when things are rough? In our church, are we a house of prayer? Is leadership zealous to seek God in prayer? Do the neighbors living next door to our church characterize our church as a house of prayer? Do they feel free and welcome to come in and pray any time of the day, including evenings? What a challenge from the lips of Jesus to us today!

Someone said, "Isn't the greater challenge to become like Jesus instead of to pray?" I could give you twenty excellent reasons as to why we should pray, but the reason above all reasons is that Jesus said, "My house shall be called a house of prayer." He is the creator of His house. He is the architect for the house of God, and He has a right to say what characteristics His house should have.

Jesus's Example: Our Greatest Incentive and Motivation to Pray

As head over His house, He is our example; we are to follow His ways. He is our leader; He is the captain of our salvation. He first lived out what He commanded His followers to be. The challenge before us now is to *be*—and to *do* it! Jesus was a man who first taught with His life and not with His mouth (Heb. 3:1-4).

It is very interesting that Luke records that the disciples said to Jesus, "Lord, teach us to pray, as John [the Baptist] taught his disciples" (11:1). I would like to note that it was *one* of His disciples. Jesus did not try to teach them much on prayer until they were ready enough to ask, but He lived a life of prayer while they observed Him.

Someone has said, "It is not amazing that Jesus prayed as much as He did, but *it is amazing that He had to pray.*" Yes, He had to pray. Clearly, this is an emphasis of the gospel of Jesus Christ. I've counted twenty-five times in the Gospels where Jesus is praying or talking about prayer.

Dr. Luke gives us the most well-rounded picture of Jesus's prayer life, showing prayers of consecration, prayers of thanksgiving, prayers of submission, and especially, prayers of communion with God.

In Luke 3:21, we see Jesus being baptized. Luke tells us that while He was being baptized and praying, the heavens opened and the Holy Spirit descended in the bodily form of a dove upon Jesus. Luke is the only one that records this. Praying certainly brings the Holy Spirit into our lives.

Luke also tells us in chapter eleven how much more the Father will give the Holy Spirit to them that ask Him than will an earthly Father give bread to his child (vv. 9-13). As we continue to read about Jesus's life in chapter four of Luke, we see that He is led out into the wilderness for forty days to be tested and tried. He fasted and prayed and had that victorious bout with Satan before He began His earthly ministry. Shortly thereafter, we see Jesus in the midst of great fame and success.

> However, the report went around concerning Him all the more; and great multitudes came together to hear, and to be healed by Him of their infirmities. So He Himself often withdrew into the wilderness and prayed. (Luke 5:15-16)

In the midst of great success, He withdrew because He knew the danger of taking glory to Himself. He knew that He must go back to the Father and receive more strength for His next mission.

Just before choosing the twelve apostles, we read:

> He went out to the mountain to pray, and continued all night in prayer to God. (Luke 6:12)

Luke chapter 9:18 says He prayed alone. Verses twenty-eight and twenty-nine record that eight days later He took His disciples to pray on the Mount of Transfiguration.

All three Gospels record a prayer of submission in the garden of Gethsemane. Luke 22:42 tells of that painful experience in the garden, where blood poured from Him, even as sweat drops, and He cried, "Not My will, but Yours, be done." What an illustration of perseverance in prayer!

Jesus's life is truly one of the greatest incentives and inspirations to motivate us to pray. Let's look at what He said as He was tortured on the cross:

> Father, forgive them, for they know not what they do. (Luke 23:34)

> Father, into Your hands I commend My Spirit. (Luke 23:46)

Oh, what a man of prayer Jesus was!

In His life on earth, we see He prayed on the mountain, prayed in the wilderness, and prayed on the water as He calmed the troubled sea. We see He prayed in the water when He was baptized, prayed in agony in the Garden of Gethsemane, and He prayed as He hung on the cross, where He shed His blood that paid the eternal price for our sin. And so, we see Jesus as a man of prayer while on earth, setting the supreme example for us as individuals.

"My house shall be called the house of prayer."

Again, we are not amazed at the fact that He prayed so much but more at the fact that He had to pray at all! Jesus's life was one of beautiful communion with God. Is ours? He always wanted to do the will of the Father. Do we?

Hebrews 10:7 and 9 say, "I have come to do Your will, O God." Jesus said that His life's will was to do His Father's will; His daily work was where His Father worked. His every word was that which His Father told Him to say. Read about this in John 14:10. Yes, Beloved, Jesus has authority and power because His life was a house of prayer.

A Shocking Statement

This may sound shocking, but I must tell you that Christ's prayer life right now is as important as the shedding of His blood on the cross. That's right! Prayer is so important that Jesus not only lived the priority of prayer while here on earth, but He is praying for us now in heaven.

He always lives to make intercession for them. (Heb. 7:25)

Jesus's life of prayer now assures us of our continual fullness of life. Without Christ's prayer life in heaven now, our salvation and sanctification could never be complete.

This great mystery has been too long overlooked by the Church. It is not even mentioned specifically in the great Christian creeds of the Church. We confess, both in the Apostle's Creed and Nicene Creed, that after His resurrection He is now seated at the right hand of the Father. Multitudes of Christians today do not know what He is doing there! The Church has not been impacted with the truth that Jesus is now interceding in heaven, guaranteeing our complete salvation with His continuous prayer life. Truly, He is a priest forever, after the order of Melchizedek, so as to save us to the uttermost (Hebrews 7:24-25, 9:24; Romans 8:34; John 17).

There are more verses in the New Testament expounding the priestly ministry of Christ than there are those expounding the well-known doctrine of Justification by Faith![2]

John chapter seventeen has always been known as the Lord's high priestly prayer, containing what the Lord prays for the Church today. In this prayer, there are several important truths for us—we can see that He ever lives to make intercession even at this moment.

What Jesus Prays Today

First, we see that Jesus is praying that we will be kept from the evil one (John 17:15). Our Lord said to Peter, "I have prayed for you…that your faith may not fail" (Luke 22:32). We can overcome the evil one. We can have victory over temptation to sin. We can because Jesus is praying for us. His prayers worked for Peter, and they will work for you and me also. Only the Father knows how many times you and I have been kept from sin through the prayers of Jesus. Allow me to give you an illustration from my own life.

Twice I have been tempted to commit adultery in my life. One time it was my own lustful desires, but the other time it was an attack from the evil one, from the outside. It came at me like a mighty roaring lion! Was I to give in? Was I to yield to this temptation? No! I fought!

I took my Bible and I told my wife I needed to go pray and fast. I went to a motel and stayed there twenty-four hours, seeking God until I had victory over this temptation. I came out of that motel room so strengthened by the Holy Ghost, so victorious in God, that I can tell you from first-hand experience that Jesus Christ truly will keep us in the hour of temptation. I believe this happens because of His continual prayer for us. He will indeed save us to the uttermost.

Second, Jesus is praying that we will be consecrated totally to God.

> Sanctify them by Your truth. Your word is truth. (John 17:17)

How many times have you and I been tempted to lay down our commitment to Jesus? How many times have we been weary in well doing? How many times have we needed God's help for God to speak to us and show us His will? The Father has been faithful to the prayers of His dear Son.

Surprise Guidance

As an example, I am reminded of a time in my own life now over twenty years ago. We waited for thirteen years for God to help us find property so that we could establish a school of prayer and be released into ministry. One day I was so discouraged. I sat in a car in California about the seventh or eighth year of waiting, and I was feeling bewildered about God's will in my life.

I said, "God, will You speak to me through Your Word?" And, in one of those rare times of just flipping open my Bible, it opened to 1 Chronicles chapter four. I sighed, "Oh, no! this is a chronology! How can God speak to me through this?"

But I started reading regarding the descendents of Judah: Perez, Hezron, Carmi, Hur, and Shobal. I kept reading. When I came to verse nine, God spoke to me like a bolt of lightning! I continued reading,

> Now Jabez was more honorable than his brothers, and his mother called his name Jabez, saying, "Because I bore him in pain." And Jabez called on the God of Israel saying, "Oh, that You would bless me indeed, and enlarge my territory, that Your hand would be with me, and that You would keep me from evil, that I may not cause pain!" So God granted him what he requested (1 Chron. 4:9-10).

I was blessed with several things in this prayer. Jabez called for God to bless him indeed. *Indeed* is an adverb, and it means "without any questions." "Oh, that You would bless me, indeed, and enlarge my coasts!" I cried to God. I was hoping and praying that God would enlarge my territory, my tent, my opportunity to serve Him, and give us land where we would establish a School of Prayer.

Another blessing from Jabez' prayer is best said in the NIV translation:

> "Let Your hand be with me, and keep me from harm so that I will be free from pain." (1 Chron. 4:10)

In the previous fifteen years, I have lived with a lot of back pain. I often asked God to keep me from the pain of my back problem. However, now this scripture was a promise in the midnight hour that quickened me. It gave me courage to go ahead and wait on Him for as many more years as it would take to find the property, which we named Prayer Valley. If Jesus was not praying for us, I don't believe we could have made it through eight years of pioneering hard times. Today, Prayer Valley continues under the leadership of Larry and Carolyn Lotz.

Jesus's Greatest Longing

A third aspect of this high priestly prayer is that we might experience oneness and know His love through one another (John 17:11, 21-22). Man craves and needs oneness and the relationships of love more than anything else. Nothing has been more thrilling in my Christian experience than to see the Word of God as recorded in Mark 10:30.

> ...who shall not receive a hundred fold now in this time—houses and brothers and sisters and mothers and children and lands, with persecutions—and in the age to come, eternal life. (Mark 10:30)

It is encouraging to see this Mark 10:30 fulfilled for those who take up their cross and follow Jesus.

Relationships of love begin in the family. What we experience in our family life greatly impacts our ability to give and receive love in our adult years.

My father and his brother, Sam, came to the United States as immigrants from Sicily, Italy, when they were around sixteen years of age. My father's first wife died, leaving him with two children. He met and married my mother, who died four years after marriage at the age of twenty-two of tuberculosis and pneumonia complications. My sister, Shirley, was a year old, and I was two when our mother died. This happened during the Depression era, and my father did not have the means to care for four children and go to work. He asked the Catholic church to help him, and it did step in to help.

Everyone was concerned that we'd carry our mother's TB, so we were taken to live in the sanitarium for a year where Catholics took care of us.

Afterward, I went to a Catholic boy's school in Parma, Ohio. We were dressed up and had to march in line. I remember my first taste of liver. I couldn't stand it, so I put it in my pocket and later threw it into a bush when we marched by.

I remember we also were in foster homes. I remember getting spanked by a lady. I was accused falsely—her son accused me of peeling wall paper off the stairwell, but he was the one who did it. I got the blame. I think most children have a memory or two of being accused unjustly. Regardless of the offenses against us, we must learn to forgive and go on. Today, that story makes me chuckle.

I missed having a mother's love. But God supplied it throughout the many years of traveling and sleeping in different foster family homes. I have really felt that God has given me many mothers, brothers, and sisters—the love of many people. To experience that aspect of His love and care is one of the greatest thrills of life. Oh, Beloved, how free and beautiful it feels to walk in this arena of life without prejudice or bigotry! To experience the love that is greater than our religious man-made doctrines that try to hold people together. Jesus, our high priest, is praying this love down from heaven.

We did move back home after Dad met and married a young farm girl. She got pregnant right away and had children besides the four of us. I still remember one of the babies coughing continuously in its bed. That dear little one died of whooping cough.

My Uncle Sam was actually the first one in my family to come to Christ. My uncle was converted in a Pentecostal storefront church. He was a humble man, and his perseverance in prayer and witnessing to all of us is part of the reason we got saved.

I'll never forget watching my dad slap his brother!

Uncle Sam would say, "Charlie Franck, you need to be born again." My dad would reach across the table and slap him!

I'm sharing all of this not only to reveal my testimony but also to reveal the longest prayer of my life.

My Longest Prayer

I know a little about persevering prayer. My longest prayer lasted seventeen years—I cried out for my dad to be born again. After I was saved, wherever I went, I asked Christians to pray for my father, Charlie Franck, in Akron, Ohio. Sometimes I felt foolish. I remember once in seminary, during a prayer time, I began to weep for my father's salvation. I felt a little bit out of place, but nevertheless I wasn't ashamed to always ask people to pray for my dad. I did this all over the country for years.

When I would go home, my dad would usually laugh at me for being a preacher and say I was throwing away my life, and he would insult me. I tried to tell him once more about being born again.

I kept on praying for him. One day, years later, my sister called and said, "Dad is very sick in the hospital. You had better come."

This was the only time in my life I had any money in the bank, about two hundred dollars. I had enough to buy an airplane ticket from La Crosse to Akron, Ohio, round-trip. I was with Dad for three days.

Before I left, I told my daddy, "I was the only one out of all your children who came here because I not only love you as a father but I love your eternal soul."

My older brother, Chuck, and I had a gift we had bought him. It was a beautiful robe. The Lord showed me to pick up the robe and talk to him about the gift. So I did.

I said, "See, Dad, this is a beautiful red robe and Christmas time is coming, but I want to tell you, the greatest gift of all is what we read about in John 3:16." I told him about Jesus Christ and how we all as sinners needed a Savior, and I asked him if he wouldn't like to receive the Lord Jesus as his Savior who shed His blood on the cross. He said he would, and so I prayed with him.

Four months later he died, but I believe there were quiet fruits of his salvation.

I know he came to Jesus because of the many years of my waiting on God and because of my Uncle Sam's waiting on God. And I think of the multitude of prayers by hundreds of Christians that I asked to pray for my dad's salvation.

And so, you see, my family has come to the Lord through prayer. The house of prayer begins in the home.

Why so little power in prayer today? Because there is so little obedience to Christ's commandment to love.

A fourth request of His John 17:24 prayer is that He prays for our hope to be increased as we grow older and to soon be with Him to behold His glory.

Jesus's prayers are a magnet pulling us heavenward. His prayers are helping to make us homesick for glory. As we grow older and the trials of life overwhelm us, our hope that is set before us is eternal life. Christ's prayers are keeping us steadfast on that path.

> "Father, I desire that they also whom You gave Me may be with Me where I am, that they may behold My glory which You have given Me. (John 17:24)

Look at the hope described in Hebrews for those who enter into prayer:

> Because God wanted to make the unchangeable nature of his purpose very clear to the heirs of what was promised, he confirmed it with an oath. God did this so that, by two unchangeable things in which it is impossible for God to lie, we who have fled to take hold of the hope offered to us may be greatly encouraged. We have this hope as an anchor for the soul, firm and secure. It enters the inner sanctuary behind the curtain, where Jesus, who went before us, has entered on our behalf. (Heb. 6;17-20 NIV)

He has become a high priest forever. So when we flee to the holy place, the mercy seat, to pray, we are casting all our hope before Jesus, as one would cast an anchor to land upon the desired shore. This anchor of hope grips on to Him who is within the veil interceding for us.

One of the most appealing reasons for obeying the injunction of Jesus to be a house of prayer is that in prayer we receive mercy and find grace to help exactly in our time of need. In my opinion, there is a very great need today for Christians to be taught an expository, exegetical teaching on the Book of Hebrews. There is no other book like it in the New Testament. It is this book that shows us Christ as our High Priest, ever living to make intercession and ready to help us. His prayer brings the power of heaven to our souls!

> Therefore, since we have a great high priest who has gone through the heavens, Jesus the Son of God, let us hold firmly to the faith we profess. For we do not have a high priest who is unable to sympathize with our weakness, but we have one who has been tempted in every way, just as we are—yet without sin. Let us then approach the throne

of grace with confidence, so that we may receive mercy and find grace to help us in our time of need. (Heb. 4:15-16 niv)

Behold Christ's Beauty

So, Beloved, let us be encouraged in our prayer life by looking unto Jesus, the author and finisher of our faith. Let's behold Him in His beauty, as a great prayer warrior now in heaven for us.

See Him as a high priest forever after the order of Melchizedek, king and priest. See Jesus as the king with full authority and the priest who brings us to the Father and constantly cleanses us. See Him as the captain of our salvation, the apostle, the forerunner, the finisher of our faith. See Him as the merciful, faithful, and shepherding high priest who helps us with His mother-love, succors us, and runs to our aid when we are in need. See Him who is called by God the Father to be our praying priest and who has compassion on the ignorant.

Jesus is wonderful, holy, and harmless. He is an undefiled high priest, separate from sinners, and sits at the right hand of the Father interceding for you and me. Let us take up the challenge of the Lord Jesus Christ to make His house a house of prayer. In our individual lives, in our homes, and in our church, we will be the glory of God here on earth for Him.

Search My Heart, O God...

1. The concept of "house of prayer" comes from Isaiah 56:7 and is taught clearly in Jesus's example and words in the books of Matthew, Mark, Luke, and John. Take a moment right now and ask Jesus what His house of prayer looks like. Ask Him what you can do to help Him.

2. Turn to John chapter seventeen and highlight in your Bible the four key requests that Jesus Our High Priest is praying for us today.

3. Reflect for a moment. Did you ever participate in a prayer meeting that you really enjoyed? _____

What was that like?

_____

_____

_____

_____

4. What is the best time you've ever had in corporate prayer? Jot down a few of the key elements in that house of prayer that blessed you and the other intercessors and brought blessing to the Lord Jesus.

_____

_____

_____

_____

Search me, O God, and know my heart: try me, and know my thoughts. (Ps. 139:23)

Chapter 2

LET'S APPOINT A PRAYER COORDINATOR

WE HAVE MUSIC directors, youth directors, and Christian education directors. So why not have a prayer director? [1]

What is a prayer director or prayer coordinator? A prayer director or coordinator is one who helps plan and direct the prayer program of the local church, or a prayer director may be called by God to lead a small local cell group that meets in a home or another location. As of 2009, the Assemblies of God has over a thousand prayer coordinators in local churches. Today there are Christian companies that need prayer directors! The group may be large or small, meet inside the local church or outside the local church. There may be thousands at the altar of prayer or a small group of two or three. The important thing is that the person who directs that group's prayer ministry will be anointed by God to raise the prayer consciousness of their group and achieve authentic, biblical prayer events.

For the purpose of this study, I will direct my attention to the prayer director of the local congregation. A prayer director is one who sees that a plan is made both with short-range and long-range goals, and one who gets instruction on prayer to the congregation and answers the questions:

Why should we pray?

When should we pray?

How should we pray?

If God is calling you to shepherd people in prayer, then you are probably already motivating people to pray without even trying! Prayer directors are just made that way. They love to stimulate people to pray! They point Christians to Jesus Christ, the world's greatest prayer warrior. They teach that the purpose of prayer is the inward growth into the likeness of Christ and the outward growth of the Church to win the lost. A person who loves to pray will find himself or herself constantly learning more about prayer and eager to teach others the priority and great benefits of engaging in prayer.

Most churches that are growing believe and practice the priority of prayer.

Definition of a Prayer Director

Dear Christian leader, you are about to embark upon an exciting journey of developing a House of Prayer. This will indeed be the challenge of a lifetime!

When does a church need a prayer director and how much time is required to accomplish this task? I believe every church needs someone to help the pastor and the church board direct the prayer ministry of the church. Considering Christ's command to make his church a house of prayer, we should realize that every church, large or small, needs to make prayer a priority and appoint someone to be in charge of this task.

Not only do churches need prayer directors, but all of the retreats, Christian cruises, tours, and journeys should have a prayer director. I was recently in a Christian retreat center. I found that there was some prayer going, but it was irregular and uncoordinated. It needed someone to pull it together and to bring motivation and instruction. I also went on a trip to Taiwan with a group of two hundred Christians. How sad that as the Church of Jesus came together to evangelize Taiwan, there wasn't a prayer director or someone to coordinate prayer for us.

Evaluation of Church Prayer Ministry

It seems that in every church or small group there are Christians who are especially given to intercession. It is true that we are all commanded to pray. Some people believe there are those who are gifted to be intercessors.

I do not find this in Scripture, unless we want to build a doctrine on two people. Anna was such a person, who is portrayed in Luke 2:37-38, as having spent her days and nights in the temple laboring in prayers and fasting. Secondly, we read of Epaphras in Colossians 4:12 who was noted by the apostles as, "always laboring fervently for you in prayers, that you may stand perfect and complete in all the will of God." I believe it is taken for granted that all leaders—apostles, prophets, evangelists, pastors, and teachers—should be intercessors. Beyond that, Paul told the entire church of Ephesus to put on the whole armor of God:

> …praying always with all prayer and supplication in the Spirit, being watchful to this end with all perseverance and supplication for all saints. (Eph. 6:18)

Nevertheless, who are the people in your church who are the "prayers"?

One of the first tasks as prayer director would be to evaluate where your church or group is now in its prayer ministry. If you're leading a small group in a home, corporation, or educational center, ask yourself the questions below. If you're considering beginning a prayer ministry in your church, the following questions need to be answered by the church board and church leaders as you take an inventory of prayer in your church.

Evaluating My House of Prayer

1. Who are the intercessors in your church? Who talks about prayer a lot? Whose voices are heard most often in public prayer? No doubt, the pastor's voice will head that list! Now write down their names and perhaps their phone numbers or email addresses here and give some personal prayer time this week to pray for each person:

_____

_____

_____

_____

_____

_____

_____

2. What corporate prayer meetings are there already in your church (include specific groups such as prayer for the men, women, children, church staff, and/or leadership)? Below, write down the regular prayer meetings already scheduled for your group or church. If there are no meetings presently, perhaps you'd like to write down a tentative date, time, and prayer focus for future meetings:

_____

_____

_____

_____

_____

_____

3. Is the leadership projecting the priority of prayer in your church? How? Write that down.

_____

_____

_____

_____

_____

_____

4. What education or training about prayer has been given to the adults, teens, and children? Has there been education to promote that all-important necessity of family prayer? Are husbands and wives encouraged to pray together? List the instruction that has been given so far. If no instruction has been given, prayerfully write down thoughts that come to you now of how you can direct couples and families to pray together.

_____

_____

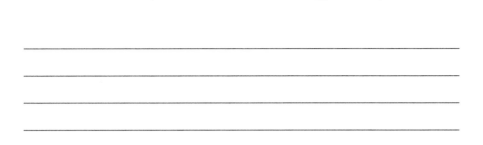

Our Children Will Pray

Oh, how wonderful to hear many voices in prayer! I believe Christians want to pray. I believe prayer meetings should be some of the best-attended meetings of the Church.

It is sad that we don't hear our children praying usually because we feel they are too young to be interested or to learn to pray. Actually, they will often put us adults to shame if we will only give them opportunity and example!

I have learned of an all-night children's prayer meeting that was being held in Bogota, Colombia, South America, where four hundred children spent a night in prayer! A missionary whose name is Jeanene Thicke from Rockland, Wisconsin, was their leader. She reported that these desperate children cried out to God and put God to the test.

One night, a young girl challenged Jeanene. She said that she was going to join the Satan worshippers and sell her soul to the devil tomorrow if Jesus did not save her that night and show her His love and power. You guessed it—God saved her and showed her His love and power!

In Acts 20:36-38, we find the Christians saying goodbye to Paul. Look at this:

> When we had come to the end of those days, we departed and went on our way; and they all accompanied us, with wives and children, till we were out of the city. And we knelt down on the shore and prayed."
> (Acts 21:5)

Isn't that beautiful? They all, with their wives and children, knelt down on the seashore and prayed with Paul.

Children and teenagers will pray. The reason they are not praying is they do not have the examples for prayer in the home and in the church. We have given them the idea that prayer is just for the adults. I conducted a prayer institute for teenagers who wanted to learn more about prayer and to challenge other teens to pray in their local high schools. They wanted to capture their schools for Jesus Christ. They are on the right track; they are starting with prayer.

Helping Husbands to Pray

It is vitally important that husbands and wives pray together. I do not get very excited about the issue of prayer in our schools when I know there is no prayer in the homes. Parents must stop expecting our government to do what God expects them to do. Ideally, we need both, but the home is the first and most effective school.

Husbands and wives need to pray together and with their children. And in these busy days, most Christian homes are not doing this. We need to teach men to pray with their wives and wives to pray with their husbands. We need children to watch this and join in.

I believe if we have a spirit of prayer in our homes, the spirit of divorce would be chased out; without our prayers, we rob God of His loving and powerful actions to help us thwart divorces. I know of no better way for a husband and wife to communicate than to share their burdens with one another in prayer time together and allow their gut feelings and true emotions be expressed in open, honest sincerity. 1 Peter 3:7 tells the husband to honor his wife so that his prayers will not be hindered. Two excellent books that I've found on this subject are *The Power of a Praying Husband* and *The Power of a Praying Wife* by Stormie Omartian.[2]

Prayer Directors Work under Authority

Let's get back to the prayer director's task. Ideally, this person would work under the pastor and the church board. They would work together with all the leaders to make their church a house of prayer. This should not be threatening to a pastor, and if you're feeling led to begin a prayer ministry, you should approach your pastor and church leadership with humility and faith in what God's calling you to do.

One pastor recently said to me, "Well, no. The preaching of the Word and prayer is my job." But the job is not getting done, is it?

Many pastors do not have the time or ability that some of the laymen have in the areas of management and organization. And, truth be told, many laymen can pray better than their pastors. (I was a pastor, so I feel I can share these points of view freely with you here). Pastors should not be threatened by this for we are all learners together in Christ. As pastors, we need to be honest and open and encourage a person to be the director of prayer. Of course, the prayer director cannot demand this of his pastor, but you can certainly pray until a stronger prayer ministry is initiated.

I was liberated in my own Christian life by a wonderful truth that was spoken by a man named Kjell Sjoberg. He was Scandinavian and a proven international intercessor who went all around the world praying with groups for the nations.

At a prayer institute in Minneapolis he said, "And don't think your wives have to be like you in prayer. My wife is not the intercessory prayer person that I am—the soldier, warrior, battling away. No, she's more like a nurse. She nurses the soldiers and comforts them, while I am leading them on into the battle!"

Those words really liberated me because I had often thought, "Why can't my wife pray more like me? Why isn't she more enthusiastic about prayer? God has called me to more prayer, so why not my wife too?" I wanted her to be in my mold. But no, this is not God's way. Certainly, He has called her to pray. We are all to pray. However, if we don't put everybody "in a box," we can enjoy a great freedom in prayer together in our families and in our church.

I am not writing specifically to pastors, but I do want to mention that it is a wise pastor who will follow the lead of the Holy Spirit and turn over the prayer ministry of the church to the lay people that he can see are qualified by some of the aforementioned ways. It is a wise church that will send these persons for more training in the whole area of church prayer.

For information about training, you may choose one of these resources that are closest to your affiliation:

The World Prayer Center in Colorado Springs, Colorado

The basic training manuals of the Southern Baptists in Nashville, Tennessee.[3]

The latest, most comprehensive handbook for prayer leaders: *The Prayer-Saturated Church* by Cheryl Sacks.[4]

Fresh Encounters by Daniel Henderson with Margaret Saylar. Be sure to read this one. Pastor Daniel Henderson has 1500 at the mid-week prayer service, and his book is full of practical tips on prayer.[5]

Planning for a Praying Church

Once your church program is evaluated, a plan must be formed and set into motion. This is a high-priority undertaking, and it deserves special consideration. I suggest that the church board or your personal prayer team leadership go on a retreat together and seek God's wisdom. A time of humbling and experiencing 2 Chronicles 7:14 should be the first thing on the agenda. Ask God for wisdom. Ask Him to heal the church or reach your community. Encourage the Christians that you know in your realm of influence to take up the challenge to be a house of prayer. Ask God to show you how to motivate, educate, and mobilize your prayer ministry.

The very first mountain that must be overcome by the prayer director is to get the leadership in unison and unity for a need for a house of prayer. Hopefully, a retreat for your church leadership or small group leadership will lead to this. Most pastors want their church to be a house of prayer, but they are discouraged and overwhelmed by their workload. Most Christian leaders of schools, corporations, and communities want their establishment to be a house of prayer and power, but they, too, are overwhelmed by their workload.

But often I am told by laymen and laywomen that their pastor or small group leader does not have the vision for prayer.

Then I say, "The challenge is for you to pray. Pray them into the vision or pray them out of the church. Pray in another man of God who does have the vision."

One pastor told me he has the vision, but he feels that the people do not. They don't want to pray. I do not believe this is entirely true. Christians will pray if we equip them and loose them in creative ways to pray together. A church cannot become a house of prayer if the pastor, elders, and deacons are not convinced that Jesus challenged and commanded them that this should be the character of the church. Once the pastor and the leaders get this vision, the church is well on its way to becoming a house of prayer.

Would Jesus ask us to do something that is unrealistic?

The word *community* is talked about a lot today. Christians are striving for community. True community is achieved through praying together. We get together for coffee, to go bowling, to do this and that. All of this is good fellowship, but true community happens when we go to the throne of grace in prayer together and commit our burdens to the Lord.

The next great challenge community leaders face is that they are over-worked. It's not only that they have too much to do but it's also that they are being required by their board or church to do the wrong things. Would Jesus ask us to do something that is unrealistic? The challenge for the church board is to help the pastor shift and distribute his workload among others. We must return to the biblical principal of the laymen being trained to do the ministry. Remember what the apostles did in the early Church:

> ...seek out from among you seven men of good reputation, full of the Holy Spirit and wisdom, whom we may appoint over this business; but we will give ourselves continually to prayer and to the ministry of the word. (Acts 6:3-4)

When I was a pastor, I would often quote Acts 6:4 completely backwards— and most pastors that I know do this—by saying, "We must give ourselves to the Word and to prayer." No, it says that we must first give ourselves to prayer and then to the ministry of the Word. Prayer is always first!

I've been told that Edwin Orr, the late, great historian on revival, said, "In the Reformation days, the Bible was taken from the clergy and put in the laymen's hands. In the twentieth century now the ministry has to be taken out of the clergy's hands and put in the laymen's hands." And that is what is beginning to happen now in the twenty-first century.

The reason it is so important that the leadership has the vision for prayer is that prayer is more caught than taught. When the Spirit of prayer comes forth in leadership, a spark is ignited. Then it is not long before a flame begins to burn. Soon the fire of earnest praying is caught from the leadership.

Revival will happen if the leadership will get on their faces, as we suggested earlier, not only experiencing 2 Chronicles 7:14 but also experiencing James chapter four, the 2 Chronicles 7:14 of the New Testament.

> Humble yourselves in the sight of the Lord, and He will lift you up.
> (James 4:10)

This humbling includes being broken before God, hearing His voice, and being revived. If we humble ourselves, the Lord will lift us up.

I was in an Assembly of God Church in Sacramento, California, when this very thing happened. A pastor started putting the priority of prayer in his workload two hours a day. But things crept in, and he stopped. The church board admonished him and insisted that he go back to making a two-hour block of time for prayer every day.

So he put in the bulletin that from 1:00 p.m. to 3:00 p.m. every day there would be no phone calls from him and none to him because he would be in his office, in prayer only, for his sheep and the kingdom's work.

There was an anointing on that church. There always is an anointing when there is much prayer. Some friends from this church took me out to dinner one evening and shared with me a miraculous story of a personal healing which is one of the most unusual healing stories I have ever heard. And it happened because of the anointing of prayer within their church. The healing had to do with a woman's crooked spine being straightened out by God. Can you imagine the testimony this was to her Jewish doctor?

The Three Qualifications to be a House of Prayer

Since Jesus commanded the Church to be a house of prayer, then the question needs to be asked: "When is the Church a house of prayer? What qualifies it? What are the standards, the criteria? I believe there are three criteria:

A Vision

A Plan

Hard Work

Vision

First, the leadership must have a burning desire for the church to be a house of prayer. If leadership doesn't, then it must repent of prayerlessness and from trying to do God's work in its own strength. One might deny this, but upon honest evaluation of how little time leadership really does spend in prayer, we are apt to be convinced of the need of repentance before God who knows all.

And what about fasting? Have you ever fasted one meal, let alone two or more, to seek God's face together as a church board? I've been at many churches and always ask the question of the pastors and/or associate pastors, "Do you pray together as a team?" Often I find out that there is no prayer or very little prayer. They meet as a staff to pray maybe once a week for fifteen minutes or a half hour.

I would encourage pastors to have at least a weekly two-hour prayer meeting with their staffs. This would not only give courage and strength to face the various problems together but also would result in the staff finding grace to work in harmony and contentment. Sometimes try "praying your problems" instead of "saying your problems." It will take half the time, and you will accomplish both things.

The Church must return to supernatural power that is encompassed by supernatural love.

I believe that the average, unconverted businessman could take business principles of success and money and start a big church, which in the eyes of the world could become very successful. They would have much religious activity and large numbers, but it would run on organizational power and not on the anointing power of God. Yet, our churches are basically running on this very kind of power: personality power, organizational power, music power, youth program power, method power.

That's all so little compared to the New Testament power of the Holy Spirit, that supernatural anointing power that prayer activates. The Church must return to supernatural power that is encompassed by supernatural love. Then the world will look up and say, "What is this? Maybe they have got the answer to our needs."

Prayer carries the oil from heaven to make all things in the Church run smoothly. In the Old Testament, the anointing oil for the tabernacle was a special formula given by God. In fact, He warned them not to change or substitute the oil's ingredients in any way. Without prayer in the Church, we can actually "fake" the anointing and rob God of His anointing power. I want to repeat that: lack of prayer will rob God of exercising His anointing power in the Church.

At some of our prayer summits, pastors have said, "This is the first time I have ever prayed two hours straight." A busy pastor's wife confessed, "I don't know what I would do if I was left alone with God for three hours."

The New Testament (in Acts 13) shows that the leaders fasted and prayed all day when the first missionary was sent out by the Holy Spirit. Praying can be fun; praying can be exciting. Time goes fast when we are in the presence of God. When the church or community leadership gets to the place of being enthusiastic about prayer, that is the first point of knowing that you are on your way to becoming a house of prayer!

A Plan

The second criterion needed to become a house of prayer is a plan. After it is prayerfully drafted with its goals, etc., a forward movement of prayer will begin. In the next chapter, I suggest some goals that you may consider to get prayer started. Better praying should start with the leaders and flow down like precious oil to every adult, child, and infant in your group.

Hard Work

The third criterion in order to be considered a house of prayer is a yes answer to these questions:

- Did you begin working on the plan God gave you for your group or church?
- Have you started, and are you moving forward?
- Are you in the midst of implementing what was planned?
- Are you "on the move"?

The goal is to be a beautiful house of prayer for the Lord doing His work in His power and for His glory. If you have started toward the goal and you are persistent, then with these three things I believe you qualify as being a house of prayer:

1. You (or your church/group leadership) have the vision, and you're proving to be an example to the flock.
2. You have a plan in place to move forward, not only on paper but also in practice; you are working on it and praying over it.
3. You are overseeing the work.

The Holy Spirit is growing your flock into a beautiful house of prayer.

In closing this chapter, I would like to emphasize that the creation and appointing of another ministry leader in the church cannot, does not, and will not of itself create a house of prayer. The Holy Spirit will be the one who does the job as the vision is caught and more true prayer is birthed in the local church. However, like anything in life that is worthwhile, it will take time and hard work.

Search My Heart, O God...

1. When does corporate prayer take place in my community group or organized church?

_____

_____

_____

_____

2. Do I enjoy corporate prayer?

_____

_____

_____

_____

3. Are there planned prayer meetings for leaders, men, women, and youth? Am I called to lead all of these meetings? Am I called to lead one of these meetings?

_____

_____

_____

_____

4. Is there any instruction given to help men and women become leaders in prayer?

_____

5. What are a few directives that would enhance the prayer group or groups I lead?

_____

_____

_____

_____

6. Is God directing me right now to plan an educational prayer program in my group?

_____

_____

_____

_____

Search me, O God, and know my heart: try me, and know my thoughts. (Ps. 139:23)

Chapter 3

PLANNING FOR FIRST-YEAR PRAYER GROWTH

Let's get our prayers out of the closets and into the pulpits so that others can catch that beautiful spirit of prayer. I've been told that world famous revivalist R. A. Torrey wrote, "The greatest trial of our day is work, work, organize, organize. Give us a new society. Tell us some new methods. Invent some new machinery. But the greatest need of our day is prayer. More prayer and better prayer."

George Verver, of today's Operation Mobilization, said, "I have never ceased to be amazed at the church's neglect of heartfelt corporate prayer." After visiting thousands of churches around the world, George concludes, "Most churches essentially have no prayer meetings."[8] Fuller Seminary reports that eighty five percent of American churches have leveled off or are declining.

Thank God that Jesus, the head of the Church, is changing this sad story so that today we find more and more churches having prayer meetings. Thankfully, there are churches arising that give priority to prayer along with teaching, preaching, fellowship, and the Lord's Supper. As a result, they are going to be great churches.

If you have read this book thus far, you are probably one whom God is choosing to do something to make prayer a priority in your local church or community. Whether you seek to begin new prayer or stronger prayer initiatives inside your local church building or you lead a prayer group outside the church walls, I'll assume here that you are part of a local church body. As a part of a local church, you're probably either submitted to church leadership or you are a member of the church leadership. Let's look at several goals that you may want to aim for in planning your first year's growth. Some of these you may leave to the second year, but the first three goals are a necessity if you desire to get moving.

1. Ask for the first leadership prayer retreat.

2. Plan the first annual prayer conference or prayer awakening weekend.

3. Encourage men to pray.

4. Encourage husbands and wives to pray together.

5. Do more praying together and in the weekly services.

6. Help the family to pray together.

7. If your church has a school, light the fire of prayer there so that the teachers and students get excited about prayer.

The Leadership Prayer Retreat

The leadership of the local church must be excited about prayer in order for the whole church to become a house of prayer. I believe it is imperative that the pastor and the key leaders go away for at least two days and seek the Lord about how they should lead their church to be a house of prayer.

What plan should be developed?

What publicity should be developed?

How will the leaders relate their vision to the parishioners?

Leaders need revival amongst themselves first.

Revival is not mystical. Personal revival need not be prayed for over and over before it comes. If we have willing hearts and seek God for revival, that revival will come. Personal revival is as close to us as the sincerity of our heart's prayer. We can experience healing in our territory today if we will come together in honesty and humility and do what the Bible says:

> If My people, who are called by My name will humble themselves, and pray and seek My face, and turn from their wicked ways, then will I hear from heaven, and will forgive their sin and heal their land. (2 Chron. 7:14)

> Where do wars and fights come from among you? Do they not come from your desires for pleasure that war in your members? You lust and do not have. You murder and covet and cannot obtain. You fight and war. Yet you do not have because you do no ask. You ask and do not

receive, because you ask amiss, that you may spend it on your pleasures. (James 4:1-3)

Oh, that we may see how worldly and wicked our desires are at times. Oh, that we might realize that lack in our church life is because we have not asked or we have asked amiss—asked with the wrong motives or the wrong purposes. Sometimes we've asked without repenting of our sin, particularly the sin of prayerlessness.

God's Word also says, "You ask and don't receive because you want to consume it upon your own lusts" (James 4:2, paraphrased). For example, you may have seen preachers compete with one another to have more members. How sad it is to see a church leader who is ego-centered in ministry instead of pointing all the flock to behold the great love of the Savior. People will attend and they will listen if, as leaders, we're more excited about the person of Jesus than the performance of our church or even our prayer meetings.

Repentance Brings Grace

Yes, we need to come together and confess how slack we have been in our prayer ministry. Some of us can repent for doing the work of the Lord by our own efforts and robbing God of His leadership in the Church. As we do what James instructs in 4:6-11, God will give us more grace.

God sees our needs; He's waiting to bless us.

God resists the proud, But gives grace to the humble. (James 4:6)

Our God will give His grace abundantly to any person or church that will come to Him humbly and in submission to His will and His Word. God's grace will be given to the church that resists the devil and sets up a standard of high prayer that stands like a fortress against the sweeping tide of prayerlessness.

Let us boldly resist the devil. He will flee! If we will draw near to God, then He will draw near to us. We must cleanse our hands, purify our hearts, afflict our soul in mourning for our sins, weep for our own sins, and then weep for the sins of our region. When was the last time you were at a prayer meeting like that, Beloved? When was the last time you experienced such brokenness?

God tells us in His Word in James 4:10 to humble ourselves in the sight of the Lord and He will lift us up. Of course, in this very passage, it also reminds us, "So not speak evil of one another" (4:11). I guess it is not surprising then, that much of what we will need to repent about in our prayer meetings is judging our speaking evil against our Christian church family.

Again, if you are assigned to lead your group in prayer, believe God that you can have revival as you follow God's simple procedure for revival: repentance, brokenness, confession and receiving of grace, receiving of cleansing, and new hope.

James 4:2 says, "You do not have because you do not ask." I want to encourage you, my friend, to ask God for wisdom for your group and for yourself as a leader in prayer initiatives. Ask God for wisdom!

> If any of you lacks wisdom, let him ask of God, who gives to all liberally and without reproach, and it will be given to him. (James 1:5)

So this is the number one priority. Leadership must seek God's face together for revival and wisdom to make the church a house of prayer. Without this, nothing will change for the better and our experience will continue to be "church as usual!"

First Annual Prayer Conference

Imagine returning from a prayer retreat with your prayer leaders who've caught the wave of repentance and revival! It's an incredible picture, isn't it? That's the vision. That's where we're going.

Now's the time to set up a prayer conference or prayer-awakening weekend for the church. Bring in a prayer evangelist, a revivalist, who will be used of the Holy Spirit to shake off the lethargy in the church. Evangelists can inspire Christians to awake to God's desire for a house of prayer. God has gifted servants who are prayer revivalists. You may know some other ministers whom you can call in to be a blessing to your church.

Christians want to know and grow in both knowledge and experience in the greatest power in all the earth—prayer. It is not difficult to keep the Church motivated, to keep prayer uppermost in the Church as Christ desires. More real prayer means more real answers to prayer. As people gather and begin to testify of the prayers God's answered, all will be encouraged and motivated to call more on the Lord!

> Call to Me, and I will answer you, and show you great and mighty
> things, which you do not know. (Jer. 33:3)

A prayer conference should be educational as well as motivational to the
congregation. This could be held separately or with the other churches in your
town. Call in a prayer evangelist, a revivalist, and set goals for the workshops.
Find out where your greatest needs are as you plan workshops. Get information about answers to prayer in other parts of God's kingdom. These inspire
the people as well as declare God's glory!

There was a large church in the Kansas City area called Metro City Vine-
yard that was established in less than a decade with more than two thousand
attendees in number. From that church, one of the largest houses of prayer
in America began—the International House of Prayer (IHOP)—led by Mike
Bickle in Kansas City. Mike Bickle's IHOP established a twenty-four-hour
prayer center because they desire to have day and night prayer.

> And shall God not avenge His own elect who cry out day and night
> to Him, though He bears long with them? (Luke 18:7)

This center is still experiencing phenomenal growth. Christians are moving
to the Kansas City area from all over the world to be part of the International
House of Prayer. At first, IHOP met in a roller skating rink and then the
center acquired a mini mall for day and night praying and a large church
facility for conferences and teachings. They've grown into new facilities and
are changing the face of Christianity with the wonderful teaching of intimacy
with Christ. This is the New Testament model of the bride profoundly in love
with the bridegroom.

Helping Men to Pray

Sometimes men need other men to inspire them to pray. Leadership must
begin to have the positive biblical mind of Jesus Christ on the subject of prayer
and the enthusiasm to portray it.

Men want to pray. Men want to be leaders in prayer. Most women would
like to see men lead prayers in the church. Jesus called twelve men in order
that He might train them. They left all to follow Him. This tells me that

men want Him to be their Savior, the Man Christ Jesus. Men will respond to prayer, but they need some coaching, some direction and leading.

If inspiring men to pray in your church or group has been difficult, it may help to separate them from the women at some of your prayer times. Also, if pastors would ask men to choose their time as to when they could come and share prayer, many would come together.

One reason men find it difficult to pray with women was voiced by a man who said, "Women pray too long. They won't just ask God to heal the baby of its cold. They have to talk to God about the baby's fingers, toes, and nose." So men want to present their petitions and have it done with. However, I have noticed that there are fewer problems in this regard with the more seasoned praying men and women.

Helping Husbands and Wives Pray Together!

There was a time when I didn't realize that there were so many unhappy marriages in the Church. It wasn't until one of my sons went through the agony of divorce that this was brought to my attention.

He said to me, "You know, Dad, now I look around the Church, and I can see the hurts and lonesomeness on couples' faces. There are so many unhappy marriages in the Church."

I would nurture my children more in how to walk with God.

I guess when one lives through such ordeals, having pinpointed one's own feelings, one can more readily identify with others. I am convinced there would not be as many unhappy couples in the churches if couples purposed in their hearts to regularly pray together about their problems. It is only in praying together over the problems in our lives that heartfelt communication can be achieved. While we were raising our five children, we always had daily family devotions and prayer time.

However, if I were raising my five children today, I would nurture them more in how to walk with God. I certainly would be more diligent in teaching them how to have personal devotions. I would make sure they more often saw my wife and me praying together so they could be helped to understand the importance of this kind of a relationship for their future marriage and families.

I received this idea from a Roman Catholic priest who told a group of us at a twenty-four-hour prayer and fasting retreat in Winona, Minnesota, "I believe that marriages would make it if husbands would just give their wives ten minutes a day of uninterrupted attention to talk." Well, that's quite a word of wisdom. Most wives I've talked to agree with this statement. But I've added to that. Let's above all, listen, and then take our burdens to the Lord in prayer and leave them there.

As a married man, I like to challenge the husbands in my groups to take just ten minutes a day to do these two things:

1. Encourage your wife to share her feelings over things she may feel upset about.
2. Pray with her—not just for her or at her.

These two pointers could save a Christian marriage and help build a foundation in your church families.

A husband should ask his wife to share with him where she is hurting and if she is troubled that day. Then he can take her by the hand and pray with her about these things.

Don't do as I did. I recently asked Arlene about something that happened fifty-five years ago. She had tears in her eyes and answered, "You ask me now?"

I was referring to the time that we packed up our belongings to move away to college. Arlene's parents lived next door to us; her mother pulled down the shades and refused to say goodbye. Even after fifty-five years, Arlene remembered the emotion of that parting. It was shocking for an eighteen-year-old girl with a new baby to have her parents at odds with her.

There are times I ask my wife to quickly tell me what's troubling her. She will say, "Just ten minutes? I need at least an hour!"

Yes, I believe that's probably true. But the secret here is to start slow. Be grateful for even ten minutes together. And, if you share for seven of those minutes and have only three left in which to pray, do it!

The point is to humbly pray. It is to start and be consistent together asking God for the grace to help in your time of need. Remember one of the greatest reasons for praying is in Hebrews 4:14-16.

God invites us to pray! While we are praying to His son, our great High Priest, we shall receive His great mercy and find His grace sufficient to help us with our needs. When you pray together, you will improve your communications with each other.

Perhaps you've never prayed together—or you used to pray but schedules and duties took over those moments. I am sure that eighty percent of all husbands and wives don't pray together. OK, but start! Start! For example, take each other's hand and pray the Twenty-Third Psalm together. That's right, read it as your prayer. Read it slowly, and put your heart's desire into the words.

Sometimes things get so busy for my wife and me that we miss our time in prayer, and we find ourselves rushing off somewhere in the car. Right then I take her by the hand, "Arlene, let's commit all these burdens to the Lord, and let's just pray the Lord's Prayer." And that's what we do. We don't say it; we pray it slowly.

You will find that as you do this, saying, "Thy kingdom come, Thy will be done," you'll begin applying these words to your situations. "Thy will be done" about this problem we have. Or, when it comes to, "give us this day our daily bread," you may be saying, "Lord, we need more money to meet our bills. Please show us what to do." Or maybe when you are having some special tests, you'll be praying, "Deliver us from evil," and you'll add, "Lord, this evil hurts; deliver us," and you'll name it.

As you trust the Lord, you will expand your faith and your prayer life.

As church leaders, we are earnest, of course, to help the home. Let's help husbands and wives pray together. What an important aim on our way to the goal of becoming a house of prayer!

Let's Hear More Prayer Leaders in Our Sunday Services

When do the most people gather together in your church? Most churches meet the most on Sunday mornings. That's a common time for little children, teenagers, and adults to gather. If Sunday morning is when there is the largest attendance, then it is probably the best opportunity for the leadership to impart to the congregation a spirit of prayer. Therefore, make it a goal to become contagious with the spirit of prayer, especially to the Sunday congregation!

Would this encourage and influence boys and men to want to become people of prayer?

Most people have learned to pray along with the pastor. However, I have counted up to seven or eight times that a pastor has prayed in one church service! Why not have six or seven people sharing these prayer times with the pastor? Assign others ahead of time to lead in prayer. Would this encourage and influence boys and men to want to become people of prayer?

Let's Help the Home

The family altar some say is a thing of the past. Families are so busy today. We have split homes and working mothers and dads. Who has time to pray together when we hardly even eat together? Our society is tearing our families apart. We must fight to keep family solidarity. We seem to have time to watch anywhere from two to seven hours of television a day. So why not make time for prayer?

Television and home movies are doing a booming business. I was shocked as I went to the grocery store to find that a whole aisle of food was removed and that this space is now used as a movie purchase section. Our homes are devouring the world's garbage. So you see, we have extra time. The question is what are we doing with it? Time is precious. I suggest we encourage our families to strive forward and plan to eat a meal together each day. At that meal, discuss the victories and disappointments of the day. We can use this time to encourage one another, and before leaving the table we should pray for each other.

Have you heard that the Mormons set aside one night a week for family night to play and pray together? Certainly, we could learn from them. Let's work at praying together as a family and encourage our church families to pray together. There is much material available at our local Christian bookstores and online to help families establish the family altar.

Let's Get the Church School Excited about Prayer

The culture of Jesus's day had so exalted their great teachers that children were not to go near them. However, the children were drawn to Jesus.

"Oh, no! You can't bother Jesus!" said the disciples. They simply followed the social pressure of their day. But Jesus, in all of His beauty, love, and wisdom, said, *"Let the* little children come to Me, and do not forbid them; for of such *is the kingdom of God* (Mark 10:14, emphasis added)." Truly our children today are the Church of tomorrow.

There are three things we must teach our children about prayer and burn into their consciences.

Three Great Prayer Truths for Kids

Of the three truths children need to learn, the very first is that their Heavenly Father loves to be the supplier of all their needs. In Luke chapter eleven, Jesus responded to a disciple's request to teach them to pray as John the Baptist taught his disciples. Jesus taught them what traditionally we call the Lord's Prayer, and then He told them the story of the man who came knocking at his neighbor's door at midnight. Jesus said if parents know how to give good gifts to their children, even though we live in this evil world, how much more will the Heavenly Father, who lives in perfection, give the Holy Spirit to those who ask for Him (Luke 11:13).

Our Heavenly Father loves to give abundantly to His children. It's so important to teach our children that their Heavenly Father is a God who gives *much* more. It is well known that many cards go out on Mother's Day from men and women in prison, but very few Father's Day cards ever go out. This shows us how deeply children need to know the love of the Father.

The second idea children need to be taught is that the heart of prayer is asking and receiving. This is what the very word *prayer* means: "to ask, to beseech." God gives to those who humbly and believingly ask! We must pray. Prayer is God's gift to us in order to receive from Him. Children must be taught the privilege and the power of prayer. Thanking, praising, and worshiping God are spiritual exercises that lead us to the heart of prayer.

The third truth that we must impress upon the hearts of the children is that prayer brings the most needed of all gifts, the Holy Spirit. Jesus told His disciples, "How much more will your heavenly Father give the Holy Spirit to those who ask Him" (Luke 11:13). Yes, the children need to be taught to ask the Father for the Holy Spirit's constant filling.

Theologies differ concerning the work and filling of the Holy Spirit of God. I know what I have learned, and I must say that these theologies of receiving the Holy Spirit when one first believes, or at Confirmation, or upon receiving the Baptism of the Holy Spirit as a new experience have not met my needs in my Christian life. What *has* met my needs is that I know I can *daily* ask to be filled with the Holy Spirit, and I know that God answers prayer. I know by faith and then experience that I am filled and controlled by His Holy Spirit. Defining prayer, one saint said, "Just talk to God out of your heart, and mix a little faith with it!"

Ephesians 5:18 tells us, "Do not be drunk with wine...but be filled with the Spirit."

So, yes, the children need to be taught about this very important prayer promise. *How* much more will the Father give the Spirit to them who ask! The Spirit of holiness, which we need to be a success in life, comes to us as we request the Father for the Holy Spirit and live in His wonderful Spirit.

A Child's Story Not Soon Forgotten

God will mightly use children in prayer and ministry if we will encourage them and allow them to pray. Here is one of the most unusual stories that I have heard about a small boy whom God sent to pray with his broken-hearted Christian teacher in school. I'll let Marge tell the story of "April Angel" in her own words.

The Prayer of a Child

April is usually one of my favorite times of the year. Watching the mystery of nature stretch and awaken from its winter slumber has always delighted my being. Not this spring. My heart was in deep sadness, and it was difficult just to function. I hardly noticed the beauty around me. A year ago, my life had fallen apart. My wonderful husband of thirty-two years, the considerate father of our four children, had left me for a woman thirty years younger. Standing in my classroom a year later, I was more thankful for April heralding the end of the school year than I was about the mysterious emerging of life in nature. Emotionally I felt I might at any moment drop into a deep dark pit. There seemed an urgency for school to be over.

I could hardly be civil about the announcement of a new student arriving the first of the week. Now I would be responsible for teaching a whole year of mathematics to this child with only five weeks of school left. The first of the week arrived and so did Danny. Within a few days, I was aware that Danny didn't know his basic math facts. I was also aware that he did know how to make friends and fit into a group. A quiet boy with a smile that could not be hidden, he came to my desk one morning before class and asked if he could speak to me in the hall.

As we walked into the hall, Danny looked up at me and soberly asked, "Can we pray for my stepfather?" Instinctively, I reached out and folded Danny in my arms, assuring him that we would pray. We prayed together that morning and many mornings for Danny's stepfather and other concerns of Danny's.

Then one morning Danny came with a very startling request. Could he sing to the class? I have been a mathematics teacher for twenty years and never have I had a student ask to sing to the class! Nor have I ever heard of any other teacher being asked that by a junior high student. I couldn't believe he wanted to sing in math class. He must be joking. But looking down into those steady eyes of his, I realized he was very serious. Hiding my surprise, I told Danny he could sing on Friday. He thanked me and returned to his seat.

Friday came and there was Danny at my desk with a big smile on his face, radiating the song he had in his heart. I silently prayed that the boys and girls wouldn't laugh and hurt his feelings. I arose, put my arm around Danny, and explained to the class that he was going to sing to us. Timidly in a soft voice he began. There were a few giggles, but then a peace filled the room. Danny's voice became stronger, and the children respectfully listened. My apprehension melted, and I became deeply involved in the message of his song! Danny was singing "She's a Broken Lady." Yet, how could this be? How did he know?

Later, in the quiet of my home, I pondered. Why had Danny asked to sing in my class and not another class? Why had he chosen to sing "She's a Broken Lady"? I did not shrug it off as coincidence but accepted in awe that while I was hurting, God had arranged for this little boy to enter my life. God sent Danny to pray, sing, and comfort me, and to let me know in a very special way that my Heavenly Father knew my pain and really cared. I had never heard the song before, and I have not heard it since that day.

A child's believing prayer is the most powerful thing in God's kingdom!

The Plan

I have stated in this chapter seven areas to help plan the first year's prayer growth. A praying church will not just happen. It must be planned, and then the plan must be worked. Yes, if we will but humble ourselves under the mighty hand of God, He will lift us up to be a church that is worthy of His name—to be a house of prayer individually, in our homes, and then corporately as a church body. We shall then have the mighty power of God to do the mighty works of God and be better able to preach the gospel to every creature in all the earth.

In the next chapter, I want to address some of the religious problems that have hindered, hurt, and attempted to snuff out the life of our prayer meetings.

Search My Heart, O God...

1. (If married) What are the best times of prayer I've enjoyed with my spouse? What made those times so special?

_____

_____

_____

_____

2. What are the possible roadblocks that sometimes hinder our group from praying? (Jot down a few ideas that may help the couples in your group enjoy praying together.)

_____

_____

_____

_____

3. What are the first three truths to teach children about prayer? What truths has God shown me about leading children to pray?

_____

_____

_____

_____

Search me, O God, and know my heart: try
me, and know my thoughts
(Psalm 139:23).

Chapter 4

THE QUEST TO PRAY: PROBLEMS
YOU WILL FACE

I RECENTLY ASKED A friend who is a prayer director in Colorado, "What problems would a church have when it gets serious about prayer?" She took the words right out of my mouth. She replied, "All hell will break loose."

I thought, *Yes, she's right.*

And when all hell breaks loose, all power in heaven is also loosed for God's children to do God's will!

Good Ingredients for Personal Revival: Two Intercessors and a Bushel of Problems.

Prayer problems usually come from one or more of three sources:

1. *Problems from within* – Most of us still struggle with those "self problems" of inconsistency, lack of discipline, and our attitude. No doubt our biggest problems from within will be self-satisfaction, religious pride with little or no vision, and a character of self-indulgence that leads to excuses that we do not have time to pray.

2. *Problems from without* – Of course, one of the problems addressed in the previous chapter is obtaining the enthusiasm and cooperation from others to put prayer first.

3. *Problems from above* – We wrestle not against flesh and blood but against principalities, powers, and spiritual wickedness in high places (Eph. 6:12). Hindrances from above really affect all areas of one's life. Examples range from breaking down of machinery, to lost mail, to spirits of division in the Church.

My former secretary, Jane, believes that one important battlefront we contend with is seen in 1 John 2:16:

> For all that is in the world—the lust of the flesh, the lust of the eyes, and the pride of life—is not of the Father but is of the world.

Jane said, "The world today is stuck in overindulgence. It has spilled over into the Church. All hindrances and distractions that take us away from the spiritual feeding of our souls and hinder our ability to read the Word of God, pray, and fast need to be addressed. We, as a Church, have a tendency towards self-indulgence and struggle with making Jesus Christ Lord over the flesh. Bringing our flesh under subjection is very difficult because of overeating, overspending, oversleeping, overworking, too much television, excessive recreation, unnecessary idle chatter, vain repetitions, and unfruitful works."

I must agree with Jane. We also have the problem that so many Christians are in bondage to fears and excesses. Because of this bondage they do not pray or have faith. Therefore, we have a whole area of sick Christians who need to be healed before they can become strong prayer warriors. The Church is a hospital! The biblical body ministry of prayer meetings is God's mighty medicine to bring physical and emotional healings.

We are pictured in Ephesians chapter six as soldiers who are standing fully armed and clothed. Standing against the principalities, powers, and the devil himself, we are pictured as being victorious. We must look at every problem that confronts us and every battlefield as an opportunity for our victorious Christ, through prayer, to do a miracle.

Satan's Tactics

Let's consider six of Satan's strategies that are revealed in the Bible. Now it is good to remember that Satan is the fallen angel and he does not have the powers of Almighty God. He cannot be everywhere at once. He does not know all things as God does nor is he all powerful. Satan is called the god of this world. He wants to be the worshipped god and take the place of the true God. Therefore, he will do all he can to thwart the kingdom of God from moving forward. Satan hates prayer because he knows prayer is the Church's power. Paul declared in one of his letters, "I have forgiven that one for your sakes in the presence of Christ, lest Satan should take advantage of us; for we are not ignorant of his devices" (2 Cor. 2:10-11).

Unforgiveness

Unforgiveness is one of the big stumbling blocks in the Church. Jesus said it is one of the big things that keeps Christians from having answers to prayers. If Satan persists to get us to feel sorry for ourselves, enter into a pity party, and not forgive those who trespass against us, he has won a mighty battle. There is no power in prayer for those who cannot forgive.

I am concerned that the Church is full of people who are not experiencing the true freedom of forgiveness. Admittedly, it is very hard—almost impossible—to forgive certain people. However, we can find grace to forgive through prayer, especially as others pray with us and for us. Forgiveness can seem like a process and thus confuse the issue. When forgiveness has been extended, the memory and pain of the offense can come back frequently over following years. If this is presently your experience, you may find help, as I did, by reading Psalm thirty-seven.

One then cries out, "But Lord, I did forgive!" Yes, but this reminder gives the opportunity to forgive again, even seventy times seven. So rejoice in this process of forgiving until healing comes!

Satan Deceives

The second area in which Satan works is that he deceives the whole world (Rev. 12:9). Christians must stay close to the Word of God or they too will be deceived. The devil has many crafty schemes to pull us away from God's Word and prayer by overcommitting our time. He plays on our pride to make us feel important.

> The thief does not come except to steal, and to kill, and to destroy. (John 10:10)

We are told in Ephesians 6:11 to stand firm in our faith so that we can keep standing against the devil's trickery and charms. The Word of God will enlighten us and show us his crafty schemes, and we can overcome him in prayer.

Have you thought about this? Satan will use carnal men more and more in the last days before Christ returns.

> But evil men and impostors will grow worse and worse, deceiving and being deceived. (2 Tim. 3:13)

We also must guard our hearts, minds, and tongues or we can become self deceived.

> If anyone among you thinks he is religious, and does not bridle his tongue but deceives his own heart, this one's religion is useless. (James 1:26)

Satan Sifts

A third tactic of Satan is found in Luke 22:31 where Jesus said, "Simon, Simon! Indeed, Satan has asked for you, that he may sift you as wheat."

To be sifted is to be shaken. Satan finds ways to shake our lives to keep us from becoming committed to the Lord Jesus Christ. We may think we are committed until a trial or test comes our way as in Peter's life. Peter was tested and he found out that his commitment fell short. He denied Christ and swore three times "I do not know Him."

To get a picture of sifting, visualize the Easterners sifting their wheat and chaff in the wind. The wind blows the chaff, and the wheat remains. Let us thank God for the shaking experiences in our lives that test our faith and get rid of the chaff. Strong commitment is what our Lord is after. Today the temptation is to be committed to nothing except self's needs and desires for excitement. I remind you that nothing is more exciting than meeting our God in prayer!

Recently, in the last hour of a church prayer vigil, the Lord visited us. We experienced some of His broken heart as in James 4:5. It was the jealousy of God's love over His people. Our hearts were moved with God's compassion and love. Tears flowed freely. Truly, God is a fierce, jealous lover.

Satan Hinders

A fourth tactic that brings problems in the Church is that Satan hinders the work of the Lord. Look what happened to Paul!

> We wanted to come to you—even I, Paul, time and again—but Satan hindered us. (1 Thess. 2:18)

When trying to complete this book on a deadline, for we needed to give the book to fifty leaders at a missionary conference, our computer disk jammed up and set us back two days. This was one of the many hindrances that we experienced in trying to do the work of the Lord.

These hindrances can result in God's interventions. In itself, a hindrance can sometimes be humanly explained. However, it is the timing of the happening that makes it obvious that it is a supernatural power in life, either blessing us like God does or hindering us like Satan does. We know from Romans 8:28 that God is in complete control. We need to praise Him and pray in faith during these attacks.

Satan, The Slave Driver

A fifth thing that Satan does is to wear out the saints. We find in Daniel 7:25 that Satan's emissary, the anti-Christ, shall endeavor to wear out the saints through a changing of the customs, the times, and the seasons.

> And he shall speak great words against the most High, and shall wear out the saints of the most High, and think to change times and laws: and they shall be given into his hand until a time and times and the dividing of time. (Dan. 7:25 KJV)

Today, we live in a society changing as never before. Even in the Church, people have unbelievably high expectations and even make demands of their elders and pastors. Indeed, the saints today are being worn out in the lifestyles we are living here in America.

God must help us to return to a more simple life and to discipline ourselves to have priorities that are going to count for eternity. Many problems come in our churches regarding prayer and prayer meetings because the saints are simply just worn out.

If this is one of the tactics Satan is using against you, I want to encourage you to plan a complete day of Sabbath rest before the Lord. Plan Saturday or Sunday as a day off from all external concerns, labors, and duties. Spend time alone with God and read His Word, or read a book God's led you to, minister to the Lord in song or in prayer. Rest. Take time to rest in Him, feel the sun on your face, and be content. Be still and know that He is God. Christians must return to having a real Sabbath day.

> In quietness and confidence shall be your strength. (Isa. 30:15)

Finding time is not always easy to do, but if you make it a priority, you can do it. Time alone with God brings great refreshing. Prayer builds us up! No prayer tears us down, thus we rob God of His blessing to refresh us in His presence.

> But you, beloved, building yourselves up on your most holy faith, praying in the Holy Spirit. (Jude 1:20)

Troubles Are God's Grindstone

A sixth strategy of Satan is to buffet us. Satan is God's grindstone. In 2 Corinthians 12:7-8 Paul says that his troubles are due to God allowing Satan to buffet him lest he become proud. Paul was given a thorn in the flesh. He said that thorn was "a messenger of Satan to buffet me, lest I be exalted above measure. Concerning this thing I pleaded with the Lord three times that it might depart from me."

We need to consider Satan's tactics when we get serious about prayer in our churches. Sometimes we wonder how these problems fit in, working together for our good. We can become discouraged and heavy of heart. This is where God is the most glorified when in prayer we offer the sacrifices of praise and simply trust our Heavenly Father's words of Romans 8:28, which promises that all things work together for good to those who love God.

Know that He is in control. Problems bring opportunity to "pray through" and have the glorious victory of God. This brings joy from answered prayer that Jesus promised in John 16:24.

In a moment I want to share with you our second great battlefront concerning one's inner self attitude toward problems. But first, I want to give you a personal testimony about what has happened in our lives since we have worked in a prayer ministry and had a desire to start a school of prayer.

Our Painful Trials

I know something about Satan's buffeting. First, our house burned down. Yes, at 1:30 a.m. I awakened and was able to get my wife out. Our lives were spared, but almost everything we owned went up in flames. Also, we lost a year of our lives getting resettled.

Afterward, a serious, unexpected sickness came upon our family and lasted another year. Next we experienced something we thought would never touch our family—a divorce. The parents, four lovely grandchildren, and grandparents had to live a shaken and somewhat shattered life for several years.

Let's add to that list that we were embezzled, our home was robbed, and we were falsely accused and sued twice.

Problems in life should not hinder our prayers; they should cause our prayer lives to grow.

I fell on the basement steps when alone, about forty years ago, when we just started our tri-state evangelistic ministry. I wondered if I was pushed because I still can't figure out how my feet went out from under me. After two months, I developed severe pain and went to the hospital. I was told that I had a bulging disk. I was debilitated for one year with severe sciatic pain. Even as I write this chapter I am in pain. I must tell you I haven't had this type of pain in my leg for ten years. It certainly has hindered the development of this book by zapping my strength. My years of back pain were nothing compared to the inner anguish that I received from false accusations from brothers. The challenge to forgive these brothers, and the victory won, were worth the experience which was a year and a half of internal agony.

Through it all, I learned to experience Philippians 3:10:

> ...that I may know Him and the power of His resurrection, and the fellowship of His sufferings, being conformed to His death.

Problems in life should not hinder our prayers; they should cause our prayer lives to grow. The problems which we had did not make us bitter but only better. They didn't blow us apart. They only drew us deeper into the arms of Jesus to find His faithfulness, love, and help.

We Are More Than Conquerors

Christians must learn that Almighty God has won the victory, and Satan is a defeated foe. Please meditate on these scriptures. Memorize some of them!

> And He put all things under His feet, and gave Him to be head over all things to the church. (Eph. 1:22)

We are seated, Beloved, with Christ. If Christ has all things under His feet, then that means we do too. That's where Satan really is.

An event in 1992 reminds me of Christ's victory over Satan when communism failed. I have a picture of the statue of Stalin pulled down. It shows children standing with their feet on Stalin's neck, playing and stomping all over his fallen metal body. Also, just recently this happened with the fallen statue of Sadam Hussein. Keep these pictures in mind as you war against Satan. Realize that through faith and prayer you, too, can topple Satan, the idol and god of this world.

Allow me to share with you ten dynamite victory verses that will topple Satan and his kingdom!

> "Angels and authorities and powers having been made subject to Him." (1 Peter 3:22)

> "Having disarmed principalities and powers, He made a public spectacle of them, triumphing over them in it." (Col. 2:15)

> "He has delivered us from the power of darkness." (Col. 1:13)

> "Now the ruler of this world will be cast out." (John 12:31)

> "For this purpose the Son of God was manifested, that He might destroy the works of the devil." (1 John 3:8)

> "That through death He might destroy him who had the power of death, that is, the devil." (Heb. 2:14)

> "He who is in you is greater than he who is in the world." (1 John 4:4)

"For the weapons of our warfare are not carnal but mighty in God for pulling down strongholds." (2 Cor. 10:4)

"The devil, who deceived them, was cast into the lake of fire and brimstone where the beast and the false prophet are." (Rev. 20:10)

"Now thanks be to God who always leads us in triumph in Christ." (2 Cor. 2:14)

Beloved, do you see that all these scriptures tell us that Satan has been cast down, defeated, spoiled, and destroyed? His ways have been pulled down and "Yet in all these things we are more than conquerors through Him who loved us" (Rom. 8:37).

No wonder Paul could say to the hassled Christians in Rome, "And the God of peace will crush Satan under your feet shortly" (Rom. 16:20).

That is the posture we must take in our trials today. God will bruise and destroy Satan under our feet as we persevere in the Christian walk. Satan can have no more power over us than what we will permit him. Jesus said, "Get thee behind me Satan." Jesus quoted scripture to the devil.

Therefore submit to God. Resist the devil and he will flee from you.
Draw near to God and He will draw near to you. (James 4:7-8)

Jesus did not have time for the devil. We Christians must learn that we should not have time for him either.

*Christians must start living as if
Satan is the defeated foe.*

Did you ever see that cartoon with Jesus standing in the corner with a big tear running down His cheek as a group of Christians were huddled off to the side, talking about their problems with the devil, demons, and spirits? Above Jesus was the caption "Why don't they talk about me?" I repeat that Christians must start living as if Satan is the defeated foe.

Jesus Was Joyful

Look at the life of Jesus. Did you know that He was bursting with joy because He knew that Satan had no place in Him and that Satan was God's defeated foe? Look at what Jesus said about Satan:

> And He said to them, "I saw Satan fall like lightning from heaven. Behold, I give you the authority to trample on serpents and scorpions, and over all the power of the enemy, and nothing shall by any means hurt you . . ." In that hour Jesus rejoiced in the Spirit and said, "I praise You, Father, Lord of heaven and earth..." (Luke 10:18-19,21)

In verse 21, "Jesus rejoiced." He was bursting with joy. You might say He was laughing himself silly. *Rejoice* is a strong Greek word. This was one of the happiest moments of Jesus's life when He saw His disciples experience the truth that demons are subject to His name and that all authority was given to them over the enemy.

Are you experiencing this kind of authority to cast out demons today? If not, you will! However, Beloved, I want to tell you that you are experiencing an even greater authority in your victorious lives! I believe the greater victory is when our character exudes God's love, joy, peace, longsuffering, gentleness, faith, and self-control in the midst of our buffetings and tactics of Satan.

We must face Satan as Jesus faced him—with great joy in the Holy Spirit. I repeat. The biggest battle we as leaders face is our own attitude toward our prayer problems and our enemy. We must go forward rejoicing and laughing as Jesus did.

> My brethren, count it all joy when you fall into various trials, knowing that the testing of your faith produces patience. But let patience have its perfect work, that you may be perfect and complete, lacking nothing. (James 1:2-4)

Paul says trials work death in me but life in you (2 Cor. 2:11-12, paraphrased). Satan is indeed God's grindstone, and the rough edges of our life are being knocked off and God's jewels are being polished. Hallelujah!

The mountains of obstacles that face us in our churches all have to be addressed in prayer, and the prayer cannons aimed at these mountains will blast them down.

Battles Make Strong Soldiers

In conclusion, I want us to consider why God told Joshua four times, "Be strong and of good courage" (Josh. 1:6-10). Why did God tell us in Ephesians 6:10-18 to put on the whole armor of God and to stand? He again told us four times to stand! God wants to perfect soldiers to stand strong in the battle that is going to face the Church. He wants a glorious Church without spot or wrinkle. He wants a Church that will stand strong in these last days. All our troubles and trials are perfecting our patience and our perseverance.

The book of Romans reveals the attitude we ought to have during our troubles:

> We also glory in tribulations, knowing that tribulation produces perseverance; and perseverance, character; and character, hope. Now hope does not disappoint, because the love of God has been poured out in our hearts by the Holy Spirit who was given to us. (Rom. 5:3-5)

Look at Paul's attitude when he was in tribulations!

> I take pleasure in infirmities, in reproaches, in needs, in persecutions, in distresses, for Christ's sake. For when I am weak, then I am strong. (2 Cor. 12:10)

Remember James 1:2 also says, "Be joyful in tests." I believe the six categories that are mentioned here pretty well sum up most of the problems we face in our local church when we get serious about prayer.

So many of us Christians in America are cream puffs compared to what the Church has had to endure in China and in other parts of the world. God is raising up an army in the American Church. God is perfecting His leading saints with endurance and stamina so that we will stand and be of good courage when tribulation comes. We are to be examples of love, truth, and courage to the weaker ones. He needs our leadership—leadership that will dare to stand in the gap and take the challenge to make God's house a house of prayer. We must pray and defeat the spirit of prayerlessness that robs God of His victory praises as He is strengthening us.

It can be done; it is God's will. It must be done if we are to be a glorious and powerful church once again in America. Hear the words of Jesus:

> Then He said to them all, "If anyone desires to come after Me, let him deny himself, and take up his cross daily, and follow Me." (Luke 9:23)

> He also said to keep on praying and don't give up! (Luke 18:1)

Search My Heart, O God...

1. What are some of the sources of the problems I face as I lead my prayer group(s)?

_____

_____

_____

_____

2. Out of the six devices or tactics from Satan the author has listed, which one(s) of them have I experienced? Have these trials helped me? (1 Pet. 5:8-10)

_____

_____

_____

_____

3. What are the purposes of trials? (Rom. 5:2-4, James 1:3-4, 1 Pet. 1:6-9, Col. 1:11) How have I benefited from the trials I've faced?

_____

_____

_____

_____

4. Can I identify a time in my life when Jesus and I shared similar trials? (Heb. 4:15)

_____

_____

_____

_____

Search me, O God, and know my heart: try me, and know my thoughts. (Ps. 139:23)

Chapter 5

POWERFUL CORPORATE
PRAYER IN JESUS'S NAME

THE LAST WORDS of a dying loved one are so precious to us. The last words of Jesus before He submitted to the agony of the cross are recorded in chapters thirteen through seventeen of the book of John. These words of Christ are cherished. He revealed some new ideas, a new commandment, and a wonderful new truth about prayer—corporate prayer in Jesus's name.

Let's define *corporate* prayer. I have discovered that people do not like this word, and they have trouble identifying with it. Derived from the Latin word *corpus*, the definition is "united in one body." It is when two or more believers are united in prayer, whether in a church or home, campground or cruise, inside or outside. Jesus said:

> "Again I say to you that if two of you agree on earth concerning anything that they ask, it will be done for them by my Father in heaven." (Matt. 18:19)

Up until now we have talked about Jesus as a man of mostly private prayer during His days on earth. We have not seen Him praying with the disciples until He asks three of them to go to the Garden of Gethsemane with Him to help pray through the terrible ordeal ahead of Him. Even then, we find that they failed Him. They were weak, tired, and discouraged. Did you ever feel that way? Dr. Luke says that they were overcome by grief. Psychologists tell us that grief makes us want to sleep.

The new prayer truth Jesus revealed was that powerful prayer would henceforth be done in the Church in a corporate way in His name as well as praying in private. If repetition means anything, then we should take notice and listen and be excited because Jesus seven times told the disciples He was giving them, as it were, a blank check to pray together and to ask whatever they wanted of Him for God's glory.

A great truth I discovered in these last words of Jesus. I have often read them as speaking to me alone or personally. The pronouns *ye* or *you* are used, but the astounding fact is that these pronouns are all plural in the original manuscript, meaning "all of you as a group of believers." Jesus is speaking to His twelve disciples, or apostles, but the message is to them as a united group. Three times He tells them:

> "A new commandment I give to you, that you love one another; as I have loved you, that you also love one another. By this all will know that you are My disciples, if you have love for one another." (John 13:34-35)

Love is the basic law and beginning foundation for all answers to prayer. We must love one another. Jesus tells us again and again to ask Him for anything:

> "And whatever you ask in My name, that I will do, that the Father may be glorified in the Son." (John 14:13)

> "If you ask anything in My name, I will do it." (John 14:14)

> "If you abide in Me, and My words abide in you, you will ask what you desire, and it shall be done for you." (John 15:7)

> "You did not chose Me, but I chose you and appointed you that you should go and bear fruit, and that your fruit should remain, that whatever you ask the Father in My name He may give you." (John 15:16)

> "And in that day you will ask Me nothing. Most assuredly, I say to you, whatever you ask the Father in My name He will give you." (John 16:23)

"Until now you have asked nothing in My name. Ask, and you will receive, that your joy may be full. These things I have spoken to you in figurative language; but the time is coming when I will no longer speak to you in figurative language, but I will tell you plainly about the Father. In that day you will ask in My name, and I do not say to you that I shall pray the Father for you." (John 16:23-26)

Three Astounding Truths

Look at these three astounding truths!

- First, He said six times, "Whatever you ask in *my name*, that I will do..."
- Second, in these *six* times He also said, "Ask *whatever* you wish, ask *anything*."
- Third, in the same six times, He says, "...that your *joy* may be full."

God's vision for a house of prayer started long before Jesus came to earth. In Isaiah 56:7 God says, "Even them will I bring to my holy mountain, and make them joyful in my house of prayer."

Jesus is telling His disciples that although He is going to leave them now, He will leave them with a powerful weapon of prayer. They are to go to the Father and ask for themselves and, as they agree in prayer together, they could now ask whatever they will for God's kingdom work, and they will bear much fruit. As a result, they will see answers to prayer and their joy will be full.

Oh, I cannot over emphasize the way to Christian joy is first through answered prayer in and for the glorious name of Jesus. This is what He was teaching. Their mighty weapon after He left them was going to be the weapon of prayer. However, this weapon was no longer to be wielded only on an individual basis. The new concept was that they would yield or use prayer corporately or united with two or more disciples.

We shall see in the next chapter how that power was so mightily magnified as they came into one accord and prayed and believed together, spreading the kingdom of God throughout the known earth by the power of praying together.

A Puzzling Question

Since all of this is so gloriously true, we need to ask, "Why don't more Christians attend corporate prayer meetings?" I asked this of a pastor, and he said, "They just don't want to come to pray." Another answer has been that some have never had an answer to prayer and they don't know much about it.

A young man just told me, "I have no ride to the prayer meetings." Another reason is often, "I am afraid to go to prayer meetings. I'm too timid to pray aloud." People are fearful of praying together.

Another excuse is that prayer meetings are not fulfilling to Christians. "They are a waste of time," they say. Some Christians declare they cannot afford the time during their week. They are too busy, too tired, or it's too far to go to the prayer meetings. Some say, "Prayer meetings are too self-centered. I only hear prayers for me, myself, and I."

I was shocked when I heard a very seasoned prayer warrior say, "I don't attend corporate prayer meetings because they are too fleshly. The people don't wait on the Lord. Some people use corporate prayer meetings as an opportunity to preach sermons while they are praying!

Where Are Praying Men?

Why aren't more men praying? Jesus expected the men to lead the way in prayer. Why is it that most typical prayer meetings have more women than men? There are several reasons. Men say they are too busy earning the bread for the family or too tired. Are these valid reasons? I doubt it. To begin with, many women work as hard as most men.

A second reason is that there are too few men models for laymen to follow. Many pastors are not making prayer a priority; thus the men of the church are not inspired by example to pray.

A third reason is that men have let the women assume their place of prayer in the family and in the Church. "Let the women do it," has become the norm in the Church.

The fourth reason is that men are innately goal-oriented. As a man myself, I can say that the egotistical, macho, self-centered man has a tendency to want to "get a job done." Men will more readily say, "Why bother to pray? I'll do it myself." With this attitude, we are prone to do God's work without God's enabling power, without the Holy Spirit's guidance. God usually has a harder time with men's egos than He does with those of women.

A husband once told me, "I get turned off with women's long prayers." Well, that is sometimes true too. Men tend to get to the point, pray quickly, and want to get going so that they can *do* some work!

Whatever our reasons are for not attending prayer meetings, here is the challenge of the conquest—to overcome these excuses or reasons. We must once again believe in God to make prayer meetings exciting and exhilarating to our spirit, to make the prayer meetings the most looked-forward-to event of the week. We must conquer our prayerlessness not only because we cannot do the work of the kingdom in our own energy but also because prayerlessness is a sin! Samuel said, "Far be it from me that I should sin against the Lord in ceasing to pray for you" (1 Sam. 12:23a). We must take up the challenge of Jesus to make the house of God a house of prayer and to do God's work in God's way or else we find ourselves in sin and rob God of His victorious intentions.

Jesus gave a direct command to wait on God in prayer.

The apostles must have been awed over these words of Jesus about the new power to be handed to them—to be able now to pray in His name and to ask the Father anything for His glory and get it. However, we see that this newfound power in prayer was coupled with the difficult news that their Lord was now going to be captured and put to death on the cross. It wasn't until forty days later, after several encounters with Jesus, that Jesus stood before the apostles and gave them a direct commandment.

> And being assembled together with them, He commanded them not to depart from Jerusalem, but to wait for the Promise of the Father. (Acts 1:4a)

> Jesus said, "But you shall receive power when the Holy Spirit has come upon you; and you shall be witnesses to Me in Jerusalem, and in all Judea and Samaria, and to the end of the earth." Now when He had spoken these things, while they watched, He was taken up, and a cloud received Him out of their sight. And while they looked

steadfastly toward heaven as He went up, behold, two men stood by them in white apparel, who also said, "Men of Galilee, why do you stand gazing up into heaven? This same Jesus, who was taken up from you into heaven, will so come in like manner as you saw Him go into heaven." (Acts 1:8-11)

Immediately, they went to Jerusalem where the apostles and other strong believers continued with one accord in prayer and supplication (Acts 1:14). Here we see them obeying His command to go to a prayer meeting and wait for the promise of the Father. Armin Gesswein, a well-known prayer revivalist who went to heaven's glory in 2001, said that this is where Jesus established the first prayer meeting of the Church, and that the Book of Acts is the result of that prayer meeting![9] The Church grew through such continuous prayer meetings. And so it is today that if we want power and growth, continuous prayer meetings must become our corporate lifeline to the heart of God.

Prayer is to our spiritual life what air and blood are to our physical lives. Prayer is the channel through which the life of Christ flows. In the Book of Acts, we find the Holy Spirit working through a praying church. Prayer is mentioned at least twenty five times in Acts. Jesus Himself said:

"For assuredly, I say to you, whosoever says to this mountain, 'Be removed and be cast into the sea,' and does not doubt in his heart, but believes that those things he says will be done, he will have whatever he says." (Mark 11:23)

As they moved out into Jerusalem, they were bold in the Spirit to pray and to do the works that Jesus did. I do not tire in saying that prayer meetings are to be exciting, exhilarating, and instructive. Why? Because we meet with God! Why? Because the results of biblical prayer are astounding as we permit God to work through us, His weak vessels of clay!

Prayer Authority in Early Church

Just imagine yourself with the early Church! Let's take a look at the declarative prayers that poured out of the members of the first church:

"In the name of Jesus Christ of Nazareth, rise up and walk" (Acts 3:6).
And the lame man got up and walked!

"...[R]eceive your sight and be filled with the Holy Spirit" (Acts 9:17).
Immediately this happened to Saul, who was waiting and praying for
a Christian to come.

"...Jesus the Christ heals you" (Acts 9:34). And Aeneas was immediately
healed of palsy he'd had for eight years.

"Tabitha, arise" (Acts 9:40). Tabitha arose from the dead!

"Stand up straight on your feet!" (Acts 14:10). The lame man stood
straight up!

*"I command you in the name of Jesus Christ to come out of her" (Acts
16:18).* The demon left!

I tell you, sickness didn't hinder the Church, death didn't stop her, and
demons couldn't control her! The first church made their church a house of
prayer. In all of these instances and others in the Book of Acts, we see what
great authority the early Church exercised. They declared their prayers in the
name of Jesus and saw miracles, signs, and wonders performed!

There were no lone rangers in the early Church!

Did you notice? The early Church took Jesus literally, seriously, and obeyed
what He said. Because of their obedience to Jesus, they were able to experience heavenly power set into motion by corporate prayer. There were no lone
rangers in the early Church. The prayers and stories that I just referenced show
that there were two or more disciples praying.

Prayer Brings Heavenly Powers

The early Church had no need of worldly "props," for they had heavenly
power. Could we be spiritually satisfied when we gather together for worship
if we didn't have stained glass windows to look at? Could we walk away from a

church meeting spiritually full and blessed even if there were no choir, organ, drum, or guitar to hear? Has our Christianity deteriorated to an aesthetic show? Instead of aesthetics to meet the eyes and ears of the New Testament Church, angels, visions, and miracles is what they saw. Their ears heard the prayers of their brothers and sisters, and their inner spirit heard the voice of the Holy Spirit speaking to them.

In those days, the Church was spoken of as "those who are turning the world upside down!" They were carrying out the mission of their Messiah and following the example of His life. What was Jesus's calling?

"The Spirit of the Lord is upon Me, Because He has anointed Me to preach the gospel to the poor; He has sent Me to heal the broken-hearted, To proclaim liberty to the captives and recovery of sight to the blind, to set at liberty those who are oppressed; to proclaim the acceptable year of the Lord." (Luke 4:18-19)

These early Christians were, in fact, turning the world right side up! Thousands found forgiveness for their sins and experienced the healing love of God. What was their secret? I believe it was their corporate prayer—prayer that unleashed the power and work of the Holy Spirit through the believers. It is this same power that can solve the most troublesome problems in the Church today.

Meeting the Needs of the Local Church

Let's take a brief look at the first century church and see the important needs that they met through the direction of the Holy Spirit:

1. The Need for Unity. Everything that pastors and people could hope for in a congregation is evident in the Church as recorded in the Book of Acts, and all these blessings resulted from a praying church. Seven times it is recorded that they were of "one accord." (See Acts 1:14, 2:1, 2:46, 4:24, 5:12, 8:6, 15:25.) They had no need to argue. They were not filled with criticism, backbiting, and gossiping. They moved forward in one accord as long as "they continued steadfastly in the apostles' doctrine and fellowship, and in the breaking of bread, and in prayers" (Acts 2:42).

Perhaps you are leading several prayer initiatives in your church. Is your prayer staff praying together? If we neglect praying together, we will be robbed of the unity that belongs to us in Christ.

2. Need for Money. Money seems to be a chronic problem in most churches. We give little because we pray little. Praying is communion with God and touches His heart. In turn, He pours out His generous love into our hearts. A happy person is a giving person. The early Church was willing to sell all and give to brothers in need. They did not seem to have any shortage of friends or funds. I find no prayers to raise money in the New Testament. There are instructions on giving money. However, there are two prayer requests about money that are startling. They are Romans 15:30–31 and 2 Corinthians 8:4.

There are no prayers to raise money—only to give it away!

Paul pleads for prayer that the Jerusalem church will receive the relief money he has collected for them.

> I appeal to you [I entreat you], brethren, for the sake of our Lord Jesus Christ and by the love [given by] the Spirit, to unite with me in earnest wrestling in prayer to God in my behalf. [Pray] that I may be delivered (rescued) from the unbelievers in Judea and that my mission of relief to Jerusalem may be acceptable and graciously received by the saints (God's people there). (Rom. 15:30-31 amp)

Second Corinthians 8:4 shows the Macedonian Christians praying, pleading with Paul to receive their sacrificial gift for the saints! Look at the heart of these believers:

> Moreover, brethren, we make known to you the grace of God bestowed on the churches of Macedonia; that in a great trial of affliction the abundance of their joy and their deep poverty abounded in the riches of their liberality. For I bear witness that according to their ability, yes, and beyond their ability, they were freely willing, imploring us with much urgency that we would receive the gift and the fellowship of the ministering to the saints. (2 Cor. 8:1-4)

So you see that the Macedonian church begged Paul urgently to receive their gift and use it to minister to the saints in another church! Here we have entreaties, pleadings, and requests for prayer not to raise money but for help to give the money away! Did you ever meet a Christian who was too proud to receive a gift? Then you understand these two prayers.

I once visited a church with ninety-nine members. They reported giving one hundred forty five thousand dollars, while a neighboring church of six hundred fifty members right across the street couldn't even meet their budget of sixty five thousand dollars. The big difference was that one of these churches was a praying church, a church with a heavenly vision to go into all the world with the gospel, beginning with their Jerusalem. Guess which one!

3. *Need for Leadership.* Leadership is another problem that the power of prayer can solve. That is why this book is so important for you to read! If you've read this far, you are definitely interested in leading or participating in corporate prayer. Prayer puts heart into our religion. Prayer puts the Son of God's boldness and obedience into our lives. It was after much prayer in Acts 1:24 that an apostle was chosen to take Judas's place. And then again in Acts 6:3-6 there was also a need for helpers to feed the widows, so seven men who were filled with the Holy Spirit were chosen to be deacons. Even Paul's first fruitful missionary journey resulted from a men's prayer and fasting season (Acts 13:1-4). Our churches and our communities desperately need leaders who will step out and begin to pray for the needs of that church or community.

4. *Need To Win the Lost Multitudes.* Perhaps you've witnessed churches that are program-oriented with gimmicks galore to draw a crowd. We must be mindful that the empty spaces were filled in the early Church with renewed souls through the bold loving witness of disciples. Also, the power of God was unleashed with miracles and signs and wonders!

What did Jesus say?

> "…[T]he works that I do he will do also; and greater works than these he will do, because I go to My Father. And whatever you ask in My name, that I will do, that the Father may be glorified in the Son. If you ask anything in My name, I will do it." (John 14:12-14)

The early Christians believed these promises and prayed:

"…[G]rant to Your servants that with all boldness they may speak Your word, by stretching out Your hand to heal, and that signs and wonders may be done through the name of Your holy Servant Jesus." (Acts 4:29-30)

They saw the promises fulfilled through people like Stephen the martyr, Lydia, Dorcas, Philip, and Ananias (Acts 7-9)! Those men and women weren't leaders—they were everyday Christians who served God boldly out of pure obedience.

No stony heart is too hard for the love of God to melt and bring to repentance.

Through much prayer and preaching, great numbers of men, women, priests, and persecutors were converted. A praying church has power in soul-winning, for nothing is impossible with God. Today, the Church needs new hope and faith that God can and will do the impossible.

5. *Need for Help.* In the atmosphere of prayer, the gifts of the Holy Spirit (such as discerning of spirits, wisdom, knowledge, miracles) were in full operation, solving the problems of deception and sin from within and opposition from without (Acts 5:3-16). Also, through angels and visions, centuries of prejudice, bigotry, and religious snobbery were solved when an Italian named Cornelius and a Jew called Peter were found praying and fasting (Acts 10). Solving world issues through prayer happened then and can happen now!

The problems that church leaders struggle with today still need supernatural answers. A praying and groaning church is a powerful and growing church.

A modern example of a great, praying church is the world's largest church in South Korea. This church was established in 1969 and has experienced phenomenal growth, now numbering over a million members. The reason for this growth was declared by Dr. Paul Yonggi Cho, the pastor, in an early 1980 magazine interview. "We are a praying people. Beginning every morning at 4:00 a.m., we have prayer meetings—Spring, Summer, Fall, Winter. We have thousands of lay groups of five to ten families, each making up a prayer cell throughout the city."[10] (In 1991, there were fifty thousand cell leaders.)

After a tour through Europe and the United States, Reverend Cho declared,

"I am shocked because people are not praying in the west. They are just enjoying the church service. Entertainment is your main purpose, but preaching the Word of God and intercessory prayer are our two main purposes."[11]

What an assessment!

Preaching the Word of God and intercessory prayer— and not entertainment—are our two main purposes.

As we Christians see the great need for spiritual power, let us offer more of ourselves and our time to our Lord's command:

> ...[M]en ought always to pray, and not to faint. (Luke 18:1 KJV)

What would happen if each of our churches had an active intercessory Prayer Director or Prayer Coordinator? We have music directors, education directors, youth directors, children's directors, and singles' directors. Why not appoint the most important or primary one of all: a Prayer Director?

> "Again I say to you that if two of you agree on earth concerning anything that they ask, it will be done for them by My Father in heaven." (Matt. 18:19)

Search My Heart, O God...

1. What is my understanding of corporate prayer? Can I think of any examples of corporate prayer in the Old Testament?

---

2. What blessings of answered prayer do I see as a result of the prayer meeting in Acts 4:23-37?

_____

_____

_____

3. Seven times Jesus made a promise concerning prayer. Each promise started with, "Whatsoever you ask." Find these seven prayer promises in John chapters 13-16 and highlight them in your Bible.

4. Father God, I come to you in Jesus's name. Right now I take time to write down a list of needs and I ask you in faith, according to these seven prayer promises in my Bible:

_____

_____

_____

_____

Search me, O God, and know my heart: try me, and know my thoughts. (Ps. 139:23)

Chapter 6

PRAYER POINTERS FOR CORPORATE PRAYER

AVE YOU NOTICED? God's presence always descends when our adoration ascends.

Prayer meetings should be exciting, exhilarating, and instructive. (I told you that I say that a lot!) Well then, why aren't they? Why do we have such small attendance? I believe, in part, it is because we have had so little instruction on corporate prayer. This is why God has raised up Prayer Valley in Wisconsin (and prayer centers in other locations) for prayer. There have been a multitude of prayer ministries raised up since 1990, including a world prayer center in Colorado Springs, Colorado. There have also been several national conferences for prayer leaders of local churches.

Do you think corporate prayer is exciting? Jesus commanded His disciples to go pray. He knew prayer would be exciting! The last thing Jesus left on this earth when He ascended was a corporate prayer meeting. He said, "Disciples, you wait until the promise of the Father is fulfilled in you. You go into the upper room *and wait*" (Acts 1:4, paraphrased). And so, the eleven apostles went, ending up with one hundred twenty praying there for ten days.

> *The last thing Jesus left on this earth when He ascended was a corporate prayer meeting.*

Sometimes it is hard to get pastors and people to come to prayer meetings. I have long pondered why. Why isn't the prayer meeting exciting, exhilarating, instructive and full of surprises as the Holy Spirit meant it to be?

Let's take a look at the preparation needed, especially by the prayer leaders, to enter into strong corporate prayer meetings.

Prepare for Prayer!

1. Prepare with Humility. I realized recently that it is hard to get Christians to come to prayer meetings because a true corporate prayer meeting takes the spotlight off of one person, or even a few people. The corporate prayer spotlight goes to the Holy Spirit, who will always turn to glorify the Lord Jesus Christ. After all, we are there to pray the heart of God and not our own heart. *We cannot have an exciting prayer meeting in the flesh.* The Holy Spirit leads. He must lead! Only then does God get the glory, through His heartbeat coming down through our hearts. With humble hearts, we can pray for His desires when we have gathered by two, three, or more in corporate prayer. Yes, it is truly a body ministry, led by the Holy Spirit.

2. Practice Secret Prayer. Jesus went alone often to pray. He prayed all night. He got up before daylight to pray. Our Lord Jesus set the example for us to be people of prayer, alone with God. In His first teaching on prayer He commanded:

> "But you, when you pray, go into your room, and when you have shut your door, pray to your Father who is in the secret place; and your Father who sees in secret will reward you openly." (Matt. 6:6)

Yes, we also must have a life of individual prayer before we can really be used of God in corporate prayer meetings. That's not to make a person feel guilty if they come to a corporate prayer meeting and feel empty. We must push past that emptiness and extend our faith for God to meet us where we are. However, our practice should be to meet with God and talk to Him throughout our day. As leaders, yet even as Christians, we should set aside blocks of time when we can pray for our personal needs

It is a great joy to be alone with God in the secret prayer closet! The Christian who meets with God alone throughout his or her week will come to a corporate prayer meeting ready to contribute from what the Lord has given him or her in private.

God is always ready with His grace and mercy to reach us, teach us, and give us exciting prayer meetings!

Prayer meetings fail because people come empty!

3. Put on Our Prayer Clothes—God's Armor. There is great victory ahead of us when we stand fast dressed in the whole armor of God. Many times over the years, as I traveled across the country teaching, I would ask the people, "Tell me what the armor of God is in Ephesians six?"

Until just recently, they would say, "It's the helmet of salvation, the breastplate of righteousness, the sword of the Spirit, the shield of faith, the girdle of truth, and the shoes of the preparation of the gospel of peace." They would stop there. They would dress the soldier and that was it.

I would say to them, "Don't stop there! In Ephesians 6:16-18, there really is no period in the New King James."

> [A]bove all, taking the shield of faith with which you will be able to quench all the fiery darts of the wicked one. And take the helmet of salvation, and the sword of the Spirit, which is the word of God; praying always with all prayer and supplication in the Spirit, being watchful to this end with all perseverance and supplication for all saints. (Eph. 6:16-18)

Did you notice all those *alls*? Pray always, with all kinds of prayer, with all perseverance, and pray for all saints. Can you see now that our armor is incomplete without all prayer and supplication in the spirit? By the way, the word *watching* in Greek means "to chase sleep"![12] This is so you can make time to pray.

I believe it is a sign of maturity if we have entered into praying for all saints—the Baptist saints, the Roman Catholic saints, the Lutherans, the Methodists, etc. All who are growing in the love and grace of God. This truly is the capstone of the armor that God has given us. Without prayer, this kind of prayer, we are just playing church. Without prayer, we have no power. Prayer is where things happen.

The Flow of Prayer

Oftentimes, the flow of the corporate meeting will rest upon the leader. That certainly doesn't mean that the prayer leader is to monopolize the prayers or even the direction of the prayers in a meeting. But if God is calling you to lead in corporate prayer of three or more in a gathering, there are a few important things to consider as you shepherd the meeting.

Come with Expectation!

You must come to the meeting full of expectation. We will always meet God when we expect to meet Him. Meditate on these promises from the Word of God.

>...I will speak with you from above the mercy seat... (Exod. 25:22)

>Draw near to God and He will draw near to you. (James 4:8a)

In our ten years of daily prayer meetings, we have learned that there is always a difference when we come to the prayer meeting expecting to meet God. We usually went away joyful, full of glory, and with an eagerness to serve. Many times we felt drunk with the Spirit! (See Eph. 5:18.)

Yes, it makes a difference when you come to a prayer meeting with great hope in your heart. Hebrews 11:1 says that faith is the substance of things that we hope for. Well, do we hope to meet God or not? Yes, we do. Verse six of the same chapter tells us that we can also come expecting to be rewarded! He loves to reward us when we seek Him with all of our heart.

So, we come to diligently seek God in our prayer meetings, expecting to meet with Him. You may find that at times you will need to build the expectation of those who've gathered to pray. Remember that faith builds when we hear the Word of God. Keep a few verses earmarked so that you can direct their faith by reading God's promises to them.

I'll never forget the brother who came to one of our meetings and said, "You know, Leon, I can't get over how much more I get out of a prayer meeting when I come expecting." Yes, he had learned this truth! We must continue to urge people to come to the prayer meetings expecting to meet our exciting God who waits to hear us pray. God delights in the prayers of His people (Proverbs 15:8).

Come with a Spirit of Adoration!

David said, "I will love You with all my heart!" And in the psalms we are encouraged to "Bless the Lord, O my soul; And all that is within me" (Ps. 103:2).

To adore the Lord is a deeper experience than praise or thanksgiving.

We adore Him for who He is. Worship is giving God His worth. We can go through a religious experience and worship Him, saying, "Yes, You are wonderful! Yes, You are Jehovah Jireh! Yes, You are the Great I Am!" and so forth. But, when we adore the Lord, we are on a higher plane. Adoration necessitates knowing who God is and seeking His face. It's when we are seeking God with all our heart, telling Him, "I love you," that we are truly in a place of adoration. Yes, it's that element of love and admiration that makes the difference when we are worshipping the Lord and entering into prayer.

God's glory always descends when our adoration ascends. Scripture says in Revelation that they fell down on their faces and worshipped God. To give one's total energy to bless God is beautiful. It certainly is a selfless exercise.

I'll never forget the first time I noticed in the Book of Revelation (after having been a Christian for twenty-plus years!) this particular scripture where they fell on their faces before the throne and worshipped God (Rev. 7:11).

I said, "Dear God, I've been a Christian twenty-plus years, and I've never yet been flat out before you on my face, adoring You for Your love."

I'll tell you, I was on my face almost before I was through saying that! I just adored Him, thanking Him for who He is—the Holy, Merciful, Loving, Mighty, Compassionate, Always Good, Longsuffering God—that's why we adore Him!

Come Ready to Participate!

We can learn to let the participation flow by promoting the *all* of Paul:

> For as the body is one and has many members, but all the members of that one body, being many, are one body, so also is Christ. (1 Cor. 12:12)

> ...Whenever you come together, each of you has a psalm, has a teaching, has a tongue, has a revelation, has an interpretation. Let all things be done for edification." (1 Cor. 14:26)

For ten years, we had a house of prayer. In the first six years of those daily meetings, there was an average attendance of at least twelve people. Those who attended learned to expect God to answer, adored God with all their hearts, and participated as we were directed and prompted by the Holy Spirit of God.

What an exciting time we had together! Mighty moves of God were seen in our years of evangelizing our tri-state area. Many thousands came forward to publicly make decisions to obey Christ.

Pull out the sword of the Word when at prayer.

Simple Directives in Corporate Prayer

Bring Bibles!

For me, going to prayer without a Bible is as unthinkable as going to work naked! The Word of God is still our very foundation for the building of our faith for prayer.

If we want to experience the presence of God, His Word must be central in our prayers.

> "If you abide in Me, and My words abide in you, you will ask what you desire, and it shall be done for you." (John 15:7)

It's so important for us to have His Word abiding in us as we come together to pray. How important it is that our Bibles are right at hand so that we can pray with power, truth, and expectation.

Forget the Numbers Game

> For who has despised the day of small things? (Zech. 4:10a)

When I started out leading prayer initiatives, I often felt discouraged because the group wasn't as large as I thought it should be. Then the Lord highlighted this scripture for me. In fact, this was the first lesson God spoke to me after I resigned my Baptist Church and started the daily prayer meetings.

"Leon, forget the numbers game. Don't get wrapped up in the ways of the world: big, big, big. Remember, I said it is where just two or three are gathered together in My name that I am in their midst. Remember that."

I was encouraged! I replied, "Yes, Lord, I remember; and that is where the power is, Lord. That is where You are present, and that is what counts! Hallelujah!"

Generally, my experience has been that the smaller prayer meetings are more powerful than the larger ones—probably because it is easier to get into the place of unity or "one accord." So, if you are discouraged because there are only a few of you meeting together, I want to encourage you that God uses small beginnings. In fact, this was one of the greatest blessings that came out of a recent weekend retreat. Not too many came, and I felt led of the Spirit to bring a message on "God Uses Small Things to Create the Large Things."

Nothing in God's creation starts with a large body. Everything begins with a tiny seed. This is true!

> ...And a little child shall lead them. (Isa. 11:6b)

> "...Out of the mouth of babes and nursing infants You have perfected praise." (Matt. 21:16b)

> [A]nd after the earthquake a fire, but the Lord was not in the fire; and after the fire a still small voice. (1 Kings 19:12)

There are many other scriptures that illustrate how much God delights to use small beginnings, small things. A classic illustration might be where Jesus took just three disciples with Him to the Garden of Gethsemane to help Him pray through that terrible, agonizing time just before the cross. Another scripture is when Gideon's band of many thousand was decreased to three hundred to defeat the enemy!

So, dear one, be encouraged even if the group you are leading is small.

God said if any two can agree, they can move a mountain (Matt. 17:20-21, Matt. 18:19)! Isn't it exciting to know we can be mountain-movers! We can change the course of history by our prayers and fasting where just two or three are gathered in one accord, in His name!

Sing Your Way into Intercession

I counted over one hundred times where the psalmist said, "Sing unto the Lord!" It's so beneficial to use music in your praying time. Sing your way into intercession. Remember the psalms were hymnals, and they were constantly sung. We are admonished to, "Enter into His gates with thanksgiving, and into His courts with praise" (Ps. 100:4). If you have a person who plays an instrument and can lead you into worship in song, that's ideal. If not, you can certainly sing a cappella or use a CD that is filled with worship music. It is so good to come away from the noise of the world and sing praise to the Lord—psalms, hymns, and spiritual songs. We can get our hearts and minds washed as we come into His presence with a Spirit of praise. Then intercession can follow.

I must emphasize that music is important all through the meeting time. Encourage one another to lead forth with a song or a chorus as the Holy Spirit would lead. Don't just sing it once if the song is fairly new; you ought to sing it three or four times. The first time we get used to the tune; the second time the words become familiar; it may take three times before we rest in it and can really praise and worship.

> Let the word of Christ dwell in you richly in all wisdom, teaching and admonishing one another in psalms and hymns and spiritual songs, singing with grace in your hearts to Lord. (Col. 3:16)

God will greatly use music in the midst of prayer meetings. However, in a session of deep intercession, heavy burdens of prayer, there will usually be little singing and probably much groaning and many tears. At those times, instrumental music played in the background can enhance a prayer session.

Having said this, I want to add that sometimes we find ourselves singing too much—as though we don't know what else to do. Singing is wonderful, but we need to keep it balanced with and praying with some silence.

You Are Significant!

I believe one of the greatest hindrances in our prayer meetings and in our own lives is that we can sometimes feel so insignificant. Have you ever wondered, *Does my prayer count? What am I doing in life to really count for God?* People attending your prayer meeting probably wrestle with those thoughts as well.

But the power of the least member in our prayer meetings can bring forth the greatest blessings. We have found that the least likely member, even a child, can be the greatest blessing.

> And the eye cannot say to the hand, "I have no need of you;" nor again the head to the feet, "I have no need of you." No, much rather,

those members of the body which seem to be weaker are necessary. And those members of the body which we think to be less honorable, on these we bestow greater honor; and our unpresentable parts have greater modesty, but our presentable parts have no need. But God composed the body, having given greater honor to that part which lacks it, that there should be no schism in the body, but that the members should have the same care for one another. (1 Cor. 12:21-25)

You are so important in the prayer meeting.
There is no one in the world like you!

Do you feel like just a little toe in the body of Christ? Or maybe just a toenail in the body of Christ? Yes, sometimes we feel so insignificant. But listen, you are important. You are so important to the prayer meeting! There is no one in the world like you. No one has your voice. No one can give the input in prayer or song that you can!

Scientists tell us that just as the fingerprints are unique, even so are one's voice prints and all parts of our body. They can now take any part of the body (fingernail, a single hair, a sample of saliva) and with their findings pinpoint the material as belonging uniquely to a particular person. Isn't it just awesome how God has made us? If we can grasp this thought that we are God's unique and special creation, it would help us to pray with confidence. Our voice will speak out in prayer, read the Scripture, sing a song, or bring an exhortation. Don't worry one bit; God will lead you. You are *so* precious to God, and you can bless others.

Remember, God never meant for you to be like someone else. He wants you to be your own expression of prayer to Him. He wants to hear your voice, in prayer or song or instruction in the meeting. He loves your voice, so use it in the prayer meeting!

It's always a joy in our prayer meetings when someone new comes and enters right in and vocally takes part.

Encourage Participation!

At a recent meeting, there were four of us gathered. (I say four, but with Jesus there that makes five. With Jesus we have heaven right there with all the blessing we need!) Three of us were praying out loud, but one was not. I knew this brother, and he was one who was ordinarily quiet. The Lord said to me, "Leon, get that brother involved in this prayer meeting. Get some participation." So, as we were praying over a certain matter, there was a scripture that came to my mind that I felt we should read at this point of the meeting.

I opened my Bible and placed it before him saying, "Here, brother, you read this Psalm."

You know, he did it, and it was so good to hear his voice. This broke down the resistance he had to being a part of the prayer meeting. We need to gently lead all the saints into prayer, including the children. That is one of the greatest challenges. They will pray if we encourage them to do so.

I was at a prayer meeting not too long ago where the young boy in the home sat with us. I could tell he wanted to be a real part of us. I wasn't leading the meeting, so I didn't know just what I should do. He stayed for about twenty minutes and then he left. He returned in just a short time and sat with us again. I thought, *Yes, this twelve-year-old boy really wants to pray with us.* But no one encouraged him to join in with us, to offer a prayer, read a scripture, or even give a prayer request. The Lord so specifically pointed out to me, "See, Leon, these little children should not be pushed aside." Yes, we need to involve them for we can learn much from them while they are learning from us.

Pray for Each Other

Of course, to pray for someone means that you must participate in prayer. I've been praying and leading prayer for decades, and I'm still taken off guard sometimes by the mature saints who have serious needs. It seems we take for granted older Christians. Oftentimes the mature Christian will remain quiet about his own needs and allow the needs of the newer believers to take precedence. Sometimes the Holy Spirit actually "puts the spotlight" on somebody. I can recall many times being moved by the Spirit to go over and kneel by a brother or sister, put my hand on them, and begin to pray quietly for them.

I remember one gentleman who said, "How did you know I had such a need today?"

"The Lord told me," I replied.

I believe that I experienced what the Bible calls a gift of knowledge—when you know something about someone or about an event because God spoke to your heart.

The Bible clearly instructs us to pray one for another.

I want to tell you about a dear old grandma at one of these prayer meetings. Time was up, and the group thought we were done. In my spirit, I knew there was something that still needed to be prayed about.

I said, "Somebody still has a need about which we should pray."

Dear Grandma cried out, "Pray for me, pray for me!"

We were all shocked. She sounded so desperate, and here she was one of the "pillars" of the prayer meetings! Then she started crying, and we said, "Sit down here [on a chair] in the middle, Grandma, and we'll pray for you. What's the trouble?"

She blurted out, "I hate them! I hate them!" Such hate coming out of this saint's mouth. "I hate my grandchildren; I hate them!"

We were astounded. She had just been to California to visit her divorced daughter. In this home she had witnessed this single mother trying to raise teenage children. They were devastating their mother, and Grandma saw this.

She was so burdened that she returned home with terrible bitterness against these children. So we prayed for her. We laid our hands on her. She wept and was cleansed. She received the Holy Spirit's love in such a way that she was filled with forgiveness for her grandchildren. Indeed, her inner healing was brought about through the power of group prayer. Participation paid off not only inwardly but also externally by putting big smiles on all our faces as we left that meeting.

Over the years, I have learned to rarely conclude a prayer meeting without asking, "Does somebody here still have a need to be prayed for before we leave?" Not surprisingly, the saints of God often have hidden needs left unsaid. It is awesome to watch the Church rise up and heal itself through the power of the Holy Spirit in corporate prayer.

Healing Love

We truly must keep healing the troops in love! It is exciting when we become honest! Oh, for honesty to prevail in the Church! We need to express forgiveness or confess, "I have a temptation that is troubling me; will you pray for me?" We need to have open, honest, repentant spirits.

> "Blessed are the poor in spirit; for theirs is the kingdom of heaven."
> (Matt. 5:3)

We need to pray away this proud spirit that's in our midst. A prideful spirit will not let us come and be open before God and one another so that we can receive healing and prayer.

Stop the Monopoly

As prayer leaders, we want everyone to participate, but at the same time we must be the one to step in if one person begins to monopolize a prayer meeting.

In order to have good prayer meetings, we must generally be careful with our long prayers. Let us pray about one subject until we've all prayed it through. Let us all pray many times many short prayers.

Other members may pull back from attending prayer meetings in time if one person monopolizes a prayer meeting.

One thing I find fascinating at this time of my life is that the older I get in Christ, I want to pray shorter prayers! I don't want to be wordy.

Jesus's prayers were short. I'm praying, "God, teach me to number my words. Teach me to be more childlike in prayer."

Silence Can Be Golden

Silence.

Have you ever entered into times of silence in a prayer meeting? Sometimes the presence of God is so strong that He blankets you with His love. Silence can express that. Sometimes silence facilitates waiting on the Lord to come into a meeting in a stronger way.

I believe that of all the needs for a good prayer meeting, probably the three to emphasize most are to exercise faith, adoration, and *silence*. This enables us to hear the Holy Spirit, and participation will then flow.

We should not fear silence but learn to listen to the voice of the Holy Spirit. The Word of God points to moments of silence in a positive way:

Be still, and know that I am God. (Ps. 46:10a)

…there was silence in heaven for about half an hour. (Rev. 8:1b)

One of the needs of our prayer meetings is to ask God, "What do You want us to pray for today?" Too often we just pray for each other's personal needs, and that's all we get done in prayer. Let's move on to pray for the nations. Let's move on to bind the spirits of darkness that are over our cities. We must move on and really learn to intercede in the power of the Holy Spirit, with groans and utterings of the Holy Spirit as Romans 8 reveals to us.

In a recent prayer meeting, the Holy Spirit wanted to lead us into binding the spirits that are troubling our children today and our homes. We were to pray against these spirits, and the leader of the meeting gave direction to do so. Only the spirit of rebellion came strongly to me, so I prayed against it. There was a pause and rightly so. We should have been quiet to listen for what else the Spirit wanted us to pray. But there wasn't even five seconds of silence before another leader began to pray and lead off in another direction.

Someone said to me after the meeting, "I was just getting ready to pray against a spirit of divination, but we went on to something else."

This shows the problem we have when we are not still and listening to the Spirit. The leader should have interrupted and gently asked, "Are we straying off the target? Should we come back and finish what the Holy Spirit wants us to pray?"

Therefore, we must exercise some silent pauses and listen to the way God would direct us in targeted prayer and always be forbearing and patient with each other.

Silence doesn't mean we are not praying. While we are silently attempting to listen to God's voice for direction, our hearts do cry out to God. We listen and then we silently or quietly speak forth, "God, what do you want us to pray for?" The point I want to make is that God hears those whispers from our heart while we are silent. He knows the intermittent listening when He can speak to us.

In 1972, a space module, Pioneer 10, was launched hundreds of miles into the heavens. After these many years, it is still operating on its eight-watt battery. By the time the signal travels millions of miles through space, the signal is reduced to a fraction of one watt. But do you know that our electronic antennas here on earth can pick up this small signal and translate it into words?

If man can pick up such a small, tiny voice from millions of miles out in space, how much more does God hear our voice while we wait upon Him in silence and say, "Dear God, lead us now in prayer."

Waiting Time Is Not Wasted Time

In our prayer meetings, we must learn to wait on the Lord. In 1991, I was part of the Washington, D.C. National Prayer Summit where we focused on repenting for the Church. The Lord led us to read Revelation 1-3 about the churches where God said over and over with a trumpet voice, "Repent! Repent!"

As we were reading about each of these churches and their weaknesses, we identified with them in repentance. If you look over those three chapters, you'll see that those churches were losing their first love; there were the deeds of the Nicolatians, the adultery in the Church, and so forth. Somehow, we got sidetracked and on to something else. When we came back to prayer in the afternoon, the Spirit was saying, "There is some unfinished business here. Let's get back to the focus on where we were this morning."

One of us spoke up and said, "I believe the Lord wants us to go back to Revelation and finish focusing on those scriptures and pray them through."

One lady just about jumped up out of her seat and exclaimed, "Yes, yes, God wants this." She was so excited that the Holy Spirit had brought us back to where we had been praying. She knew the group got sidetracked, but she was hesitant to speak up. So, we must stay focused and have laser-beam prayer, like the guided missiles that helped win the Persian Gulf War. Get the Holy Spirit's direction on how He would have you or your group pray. Then bombard heaven over that subject until it's "prayed through." Only then go on to pray for something else. We need to steer away from "shotgun prayers."

Each prayer meeting is a special symphony of the Holy Spirit. He is the conductor, and we are His instruments!

Yes, we must learn to be silent and wait on the Lord, get the mind of God, and then pray about what He reveals. Each person present can pray a short prayer—or many short prayers—about the same thing. That becomes exciting when our voices, many voices, are heard. Each prayer meeting is a special symphony of the Holy Spirit. He is the conductor and we are His instruments! Heaven is robbed without His symphony of corporate prayers.

An Awesome Prayer Meeting

I want to conclude this chapter by sharing with you about one of the most awesome prayer meetings that happened during a prayer summit. There were about twenty of us and a time of much weeping. The Lord said for some of us to lie on the floor, as it says in Joel chapter two—preachers, pastors, elders— and come before the altar and weep and fast and pray for the body. And so we were on our faces for over an hour. I felt like something was being birthed as we prayed for the church. God gave us a Word in James chapter four, and so we prayed that section aloud.

We saw that the wisdom of the world results in so much division, bitterness, envy, and strife in the Church. This worldly wisdom is sinful and devilish as James 3:15 tells us. We were praying for the James 3:17 wisdom—the wisdom from above that is first pure and then peaceable—to come on the church and the pastors.

> Now the fruit of righteousness is sown in peace by those who make peace. (James 3:18)

We began to say, "The fruit of righteousness be over Washington, D.C. and over the church here." I don't know how many times that phrase "the fruit of righteousness" was called out, shouted out, prayed, bawled out, but we saw the Holy Spirit put His finger on the phrase and so we followed suit! One could definitely sense the reality of being in a spiritual battle with the Word of God breaking down strongholds.

My friend, we can't go wrong when we pray the Word. That's why I say we must come to the prayer meeting with our Bibles. Let the Lord lead us with the Word in our prayers, and our little prayer meetings can expand to one-, two-, three-hour prayer meetings with no hardship at all.

There is such joy when we know we've been interceding dressed in the whole armor of God. We have truly put on the capstone of the armor of God when we've been praying always with all prayer and supplication in the Spirit for all the saints. We can know we've been making history. We can know we are helping the church be a house of prayer for all nations.

Let us pray that this would be true. Our church, and all the Christian churches, will again become houses of prayer for all nations, that the world will see that we belong to Jesus Christ, the greatest prayer warrior earth has ever known. Our prayer warrior on earth and, hallelujah, He is still at it in heaven for us now!

Search My Heart, O God...

1. Take a moment right now to practice waiting time in prayer. Engage in silence. Did God speak to your heart? Did you find a higher level of peace and trust? Write your experience here:

_____

_____

_____

_____

2. Is Ephesians 6:10-19 written to one person or to the whole church? _____ How does the corporate body, together, put on the whole armor of God?

_____

_____

_____

_____

3. What do I expect, as a prayer leader and intercessor, when I call together a prayer meeting?

_____

_____

_____

_____

Search me, O God, and know my heart: try me, and know my thoughts. (Ps. 139:23)

Chapter 7

SEVEN DEADLY PRACTICES THAT WILL KILL PRAYER MEETINGS

A T THE RISK of sounding negative, I want to share some reasons why thousands of churches have buried their prayer meetings. Seven deadly things that kill prayer meetings are:

1. Long talks
2. Long prayers
3. Long sharing times
4. No prayers
5. No fervency
6. No tears or burden for lost souls
7. No world vision

1. Long Talks. Did you ever stop a speaker in the middle of his teaching and say, "Could we pray now?" I did once.

It was in California, and we were having a deeper life retreat weekend. I was with well-known retreat speaker Campbell MacAlpine at a 6:00 a.m. prayer meeting. To our dismay, a gentleman got up and began giving a very long teaching. We both began to get extremely squirmy as the moments rolled by.

MacAlpine leaned over to me and said, "I thought this was to be a prayer meeting."

I shrugged my shoulders and said, "I thought it was too."

We both sat there a little longer until I waved my hand at the end of one of his sentences and indicated that we really had a lot of prayer burdens that we would like to take before the Lord. I wondered if we could use the rest of the time in prayer. The gentleman cut his time short, and we were able to begin praying!

This is an example of what sometimes goes on in our churches today in our prayer meetings. The mid-week prayer meeting has all but died and gone the way of history. If a church is meeting on Wednesday, the name of the service has been changed to "Bible Study" or "Family Night," and rightly so because there has been so little prayer in the midweek service. Even so, it is not uncommon to go to a prayer meeting where half of the time or more is given to Bible study and most of the time is given to things unrelated to prayer.

Now, we need Bible study. At the same time, we must be aware of giving time for prayer. We need to understand our people and be able to discern where they are as to how long they can pray. As we begin with one hour or so and grow into two and three hours, we find the time goes so quickly in the presence of God.

I was asked to lead an evening one-hour prayer meeting a year or so ago. I was aware that the pastor always prepared a talk, and so I prepared a Bible study also. Somewhere in the midst of our discussion of what it meant to pray in Jesus's name, a woman indicated that she had come to pray and not to discuss. Well, she was right, and the next week when we met, we spent the whole hour before the Lord.

People do want to pray. People want to learn to pray. If prayer leaders rise up to lead and guide them, they will learn. We can all say with Paul, "I don't know how to pray, but the Holy Spirit in me is praying (Rom. 8:26, paraphrased)." We are all learners, so let's beware of the long talks that dampen the spirit of prayer and rob prayer time.

2. Long Prayers. Solos have their place in the choir, and long prayers have their place in some meetings. However, if you have a limited time to pray, it is so much better that each pray three or four short prayers over the burden that is before the group than to have one or two long prayers pray.

As a pastor myself, I must admit that most of us pastors have been the guiltiest of this in our churches with the deacons and elders running a close second! They have learned from the pastor to pray 1-o-n-g prayers! Long prayers have their place, but not generally in a corporate prayer meeting where everyone should pray. Let us basically keep our long prayers for our secret closet when we're alone with the Lord. Even then we should take some deep breaths and be still so God has the opportunity to speak to us.

A lot of the excitement in a prayer meeting comes from waiting on God in order to pray His heart. We need to take time to listen and "tune in" to God's agenda. It's easy to bring "hurriedness" into the prayer meeting and "rattle on." A wise leader will get the group to settle down and settle into God's presence before praying. This is not difficult and is learned by taking a little time to wait on God. The other very important ingredient is to be willing to participate with prayers which are short and to the point. No one person should monopolize the meeting. That is the Holy Spirit's job!

3. Long Sharing Times. The prayer meeting was scheduled to start at seven o'clock, and we must be honest and say that it's no surprise when it begins six minutes late. Perhaps there is a lot of uninteresting and unrelated talk going on. This often happens just to kill time or to fellowship and wait on latecomers. Sometimes the leader will engage in song and prayer requests and praise reports. This can go on for quite some time until prayer begins at seven forty six. This means we talked for forty minutes! You have to do what the Lord is showing you to do with your group. But everyone knows—talking to each other is not nearly as exciting as talking to God!

When time is limited, pray it, don't say it!

When we come to a prayer meeting, we've come primarily to talk to God, and not to each other. There is certainly time to minister to one another in prayer. However, talking to each other for a long time about our burdens sometimes quenches the Holy Spirit and hinders the meeting.

4. Too Timid to Pray. Fear of how one will sound is one of the biggest reasons for silence in a prayer meeting. I once had this problem in the Presbyterian church I pastored while I was a seminary student. To help these Christians with their timidity and fear, I wrote out prayer requests that were given. I told each of the timid people to read the prayer requests out loud to us. This helped once they heard their voices speaking prayer. Short prayers were encouraged—even one-sentence prayers. The silent prayers began to take part once they began to pray short prayers.

It is perfectly all right to teach the timid to pray only part of the Lord's Prayer as you begin. You can say, "Lord, let your will be done in this situation. Father, deliver me from the evil of such and such." If we teach with these short prayers, they will soon know and experience the great power that is in their midst. I have experienced great joy in helping the timid begin to pray. Sometimes I've just had them read The Lord's Prayer in and lead the whole group in praying The Lord's Prayer. As they respond to this encouragement, they bring joy to all present too. People really do want to pray, but long sharing and long prayers hinder the timid. A great teaching tool to help on this subject is the classic book *What Happens When Women Pray?* by Evelyn Christensen and Viola Blake.[13]

5. No Fervency. James, the brother of Jesus, writes, "The effective fervent prayer of a righteous man avails much" (James 5:16).

Beware of the barrenness of passion and tears in our prayer meetings.

How refreshing and exciting to hear prayers with passion, fervency, and even tears. James infers that prayer is serious business. Prayer is more than communion with God. Prayer is an urgent asking and receiving from the Father's heart. How wonderful it is that our Lord Jesus wept and was fervent in prayer. In the book of Hebrews, chapter five, we read that Jesus prayed with strong crying and tears.

Do you know a Christian who's backslidden? The Hebrew root word for *backslider* means "to go in a circle." When we see loved ones and friends wasting their lives, just going in circles away from God, we will get more fervent and hopefully have more faith to pray as we claim this promise:

> If anyone sees his brother sinning a sin which does not lead to death, he will ask, and He will give him life for those who commit sin not leading to death. (1 John 5:16)

Prayer inoculates the backslider with life.

When the disciples asked Jesus to teach them to pray, Jesus gave them the story of a man who unashamedly begged his neighbor for bread at midnight. Jesus said it was because of his fervent, shameless, and persistent asking that his prayer was answered. We must shake off our lethargy! We must shake off our nice, quiet, and comfortable prayers and cry out with more fervency and compassion. God will answer! He loves us!

6. *No Prayers and Tears for the Lost.* I was so excited to walk into a Roman Catholic church in Old Towne, Albuquerque, and find a bulletin posted that read, "Prayer meeting Friday night. Come pray for lost souls." This is what the Church is all about—to take the good news to hurting and broken humanity! Something breaks in the heavenlies when men and women shed tears for the lost.

My brother-in-law, Bob, drove one hundred twenty miles to witness to my wife, Arlene, and me. I laughed at him when he told us, "Leon, you must be born again."

He challenged us to simply ask God if what he was saying was true. He said, "Lee, we believed and gave our hearts to Jesus and we are forgiven and changed."

Yes, he was changed. Instead of swear words, he was using Bible words. However, he said something that we could not forget. He said something that gripped our hearts.

Bob said, "There is a little Baptist church in Spartansburg, Pennsylvania, where a group of people are meeting tonight, and they are praying for you to turn your life over to the Lord Jesus Christ and experience His salvation."

We were deeply touched that people we didn't know were praying for us. So, Arlene and I asked God for three nights if this Calvary story was true. We were convicted of our sins, so we got out of bed and knelt, repenting, and giving our hearts to the Lord. With that simple little prayer, the power and glory of Jesus Christ came into our lives and we began an adventure full of miracles by being a family that was a "House of Prayer."

My sister Shirley is one year younger than I—and I started witnessing to her right away. She was a good Catholic and had been to Catholic school. I led her to the Lord in our kitchen. Afterward, she quickly walked to her Catholic priest and asked him "Why haven't you told me that God loved me so much and that I could be saved and know that I am completely forgiven of my past and know now I have eternal life?"

The priest replied, "Don't you think you will ever sin again?"

She stopped going to the Catholic church and was baptized about a month later.

Shirley's response so blessed me I felt that this is what I wanted to spend the rest of my life doing, helping people come to know Jesus as their Savior and Lord.

It was around that time that I went to my older sister's home, knocked on her door, and exclaimed, "Hazel, I got saved, and I know you could put a butcher knife right into my heart and I would go straight to heaven." Of course I was put out a little bit at the time and wondered why she wasn't more receptive!

Guys at work were laughing at me and calling me the preacher, but God was smiling at me and calling to me to be His fulltime servant.

I am always touched when I hear someone pray for a needy soul. This puts Jesus Christ's life into the prayer meeting, for He came to seek and save the lost.

Those who sow in tears shall reap in joy. (Ps. 126:5)

For as soon as Zion was in labor, she gave birth to her children. (Isa. 66:8)

Prayers, tears, and a burden from heaven for lost souls are the things that bring a prayer meeting to life! This is the very heart of why we have prayer meetings, the very heart of why the Church exists, and the highest fruit of what we can see manifested through our fervent prayer meetings.

May God give us such a burden of prayer for lost souls today.

And as it is appointed for men to die once, but after this the judgment. (Heb. 9:27)

7. No World Vision. Variety generally adds to the excitement of the prayer meeting. A wise leader will bring into the prayer meeting the needs of other Christians outside the individuals attending the prayer meeting. It is very common and good to pray for ourselves, our loved ones, and our city; that is our Jerusalem. But we need to reach out. We need to get a sense of being world Christians who have brothers and sisters in other lands that desire and need our prayers. In Hebrews 13:3 we are called on to pray for the suffering Christians and remember those who suffer as those who suffer with them.

Religion that is undefiled before God the Father is to visit the widows and the orphans. Think of the thousands of orphaned street children in Mexico

City for instance. Think of the thousands of hungry children in other lands and other cities sleeping on the streets. Our hearts need to go outside the four walls of our church. Today's internet access helps us to find the needs of widows, orphans, and the missionaries who care for them on a day to day basis.

World Mission's online statistics report that in 1976 there were seventeen thousand unreached people groups. As of 2010, there were approximately six thousand unreached people groups who have no gospel witness.[14]

Think of this. There are four hundred thousand churches in America and six thousand unreached people groups. If you divide the needed people by the number of churches, we arrive at the fact that fifty-seven churches in America could combine together and target one lost people group to get the gospel to them. Fifty-seven churches could surely rouse enough prayer support and enough financial support to reach just one group.

Search My Heart, O God...

1. As I read the seven practices that are detrimental to corporate prayer, was there one (or more) that I identified with in my group? Which one(s)?

_____

_____

_____

_____

2. Has the Lord shown me what to do about any hindrances to prayer in my group? Are there changes I should make?

_____

_____

_____

_____

3. Are there additional practices in prayer that are hindering prayer meetings that I lead?

_____

_____

_____

_____

Search me, O God, and know my heart: try
me, and know my thoughts. (Ps. 139:23)

Chapter 8

PRINCIPLES FOR PRAYING TOGETHER WITH POWER

The Need for an Appointed Leader

Corporate prayer meetings need a leader! I believe you've chosen to read this book because God is calling you to pray individually or corporately. There are times when mature Christians gather for prayer and each one is trained to allow the Holy Spirit to lead, and so it happens beautifully. Such refreshing times when everyone present is led by Him!

However, most prayer gatherings have a mixture of the mature saints and new Christians. Have you ever gone to a prayer meeting only to sit around chattering and wondering when is this going to start, or who is suppose to start it? I have had many such frustrating experiences over the years.

A person called to lead in prayer will start the meeting, gently guide the meeting, and close the meeting. It is important in attempting to get participation that the leader be as low-keyed in the background as possible. However, his or her presence is vital to the group as a whole and to the ministry of the Holy Spirit in prayer.

In guiding a meeting, a leader must follow the guidance of the Holy Spirit—but you want to begin and close at the stated time. The people will come to trust you and want to attend if they know there is a framework for prayer. We must be mindful that prayer warriors who attend prayer times have families, schedules, and responsibilities. We need to respect their time and use it as wisely as possible. If it is an open-ended meeting, with no set time to close, then remind people that they may quietly leave when they need to leave and then close the meeting when you sense that the season of prayer has finished.

If there is a special purpose for the meeting, it should be stated. A leader must always point people to the Lord Jesus Christ. The leader may use scriptures like these to begin the meeting:

> *The Lord is near to all who call upon Him, to all who call upon Him in truth. (Ps. 145:18)*

Enter His gates with thanksgiving, and into His courts with praise. (Ps. 100:4)

Again, you will want to begin and close at the stated time. Almost always it is wise to close by increasing a sense of solidarity and belonging to the family of God. One way is to form a circle and hold hands. However, be aware that some people do not like holding hands. You can't go wrong by quoting a scriptural benediction or singing a glory song such as "All Hail the Power of Jesus' Name." A leader is to lead and to guide. Without leaders in prayer meetings, there is little sense of direction and solidarity.

The Need for Unity

One of the most important things a leader can do is unite the group. What did Jesus say?

Again I say to you that if two of you agree on earth concerning anything that they ask, it will be done for them by My Father in heaven. (Matt. 18:19)

Jesus said six times to His disciples: *"If you ask anything in My name, I will do it. (John 14:14)*

In the Book of Acts, they were in one accord. They had the same mind about what they were praying. They were in unity of heart and mind. This is so important when we come to pray.

Sometimes I like to bring a new group into unity by leading them in this following confession:

1. Father, in the name of Jesus, we confess that we love You; that Jesus Christ is our Lord and Savior.

2. We confess together that we desire to obey Your Word and especially Your Son's new commandment. He repeated five times, "A new commandment I give to you, that you love one another; as I have loved you, that you also love one another" (John 13:34). And so, we confess that we love each other regardless of our doctrinal differences.

3. We confess together that God's work is done not by might, not power, but by God's spirit. We confess that we come to obey His Word and to pray in the name of Jesus in order to see problems that are like mountains cast into the sea.

4. We confess that we want to be clean vessels, and so we ask the Holy Spirit to search our hearts. When we confess that we are of one heart and of one spirit, great power will come into our prayer meetings.

Laser-Beam Theme

I was privileged to be a part of daily prayer meetings for ten years. Something exciting began to happen in those daily prayer meetings. We discovered that usually a theme emerged and that we were to pray through on this theme until it was covered. In the Persian Gulf War, laser-beam bombs were introduced. A very specific target was to be destroyed. So it should be in many of our prayer meetings that the Holy Spirit leads us to pray for the lost, the government, college students, a nation, or a specific problem that is before us.

It is exciting to feel the Holy Spirit draw out prayer about one specific subject. I remember when I was working and going to seminary in South Dakota and money was so tight. One day, in despair, I knelt at the couch with my seven-year-old son and prayed for God's help and provision. We said, "Amen," and we heard a noise at the door.

We went to the door to find two envelopes with two checks from two separate states (Ohio and Pennsylvania) in the mail totaling around $200—a lifeline for us at that time.

Another time, we had a rather amusing answer to prayer for food. The neighbor's 12-year-old boy surprised us and carried into our home two ducks that his dad shot while hunting! I said, "I don't know how to clean ducks!," but the boy eagerly offered to clean them for us. (My son was four at the time, and he reminded me to include this story in the book!) Well, God sent meat to the Jews in the wilderness, so who am I to be picky about how God chooses to send dinner?

We can do the same thing when we're leading a group of people—we can bring a specific need to the forefront and pray with faith for that need to be met. This requires sensitivity and listening, but you know when the Lord is leading you by His Spirit. You can also sense when you are not finished praying on a theme. You still need to cry out to God and continue to draw out more prayer.

Often in our prayer meetings, our prayers seem to be shot from BB guns going all over instead of being concentrated on one target. This brings a sense of uncertainty and a lack of power. When we pray in laser-beam fashion, we zero in on a target and pray until a sense of mission is accomplished. The leader can then urge us to go on. This brings a sense of unity, power, and joy in our prayer meetings.

Go with the Flow

The next powerful principle would be to "go with the flow." With God's help, we can know when to merge, pray, obey the spirit, and be quiet.

There are shorter prayer meetings when you don't expect a special theme to develop. You are there to pray for guidance, protection, maybe just a general blessing, or a goodbye prayer. However, in a prayer meeting of an hour or more, it takes restraint to be still, listen, and discern the flow of the Holy Spirit and where He is taking the prayer meeting.

God is an orderly God, and He handles one thing at a time. There should be a flow of praise and worship, repentance, some personal petitions, intercession, and victory praise. Listen with your spiritual ears and go with God's flow in the prayer meeting. It is better to be still than to interrupt the flow. At some Prayer Summit meetings with pastors, we at first encouraged prayers not to pray until they asked God three times, "Lord, should I offer this prayer now?"

Learning to go with the flow is like any other skill. The more you practice, the better you get. Soon it will become second nature to you to hear the voice of God in your spirit. Just take your first step, and the other steps will come easily.

Our Best for God's Best

Give God your best planning for group prayer meetings. Use your best instrumentalists, singers, and in some cases, the best choir. We must destroy our subconscious thoughts that prayer meetings are not worthy of our best efforts and that few will come. Also, reject the lie that people don't want to pray. Is our best only for Sunday morning? When Christians come to minister for the church body, would they sing or play their instruments even if they knew that only Jesus would be there? This is the attitude we must have for a prayer meeting. Give God our best.

Bob Willhite, who founded Prayer Embassy in Washington, D.C., has suggested that we take time to plan for prayer for some of our Sunday services as much as we plan our worship time or even the time it takes to make out the bulletin. How much time do we plan for prayer in our Sunday morning services? He suggests that if we have an hour and a half service, why not give the Lord a third of that time for the Word of God, a third for worship, and a third for prayer. Why not?

One answer will be, "Well, we are trying to reach the lost." And my response to that is that our seeker-sensitive services would be more effective if the seeker could hear friends or strangers praying for their loved ones' needs. I know that it impacted me when my brother-in-law told us that there was a group of people praying for us.

Bob Willhite suggests choosing maybe ten different people, picked out earlier in the week, to lead in a three-minute prayer during the Sunday morning service. You can even give them the subject to pray about. Now wouldn't this be great to have ten different people praying passionately for various requests instead of just one prayer?

Physical Facilities are Important

God wants to pour out His spirit of prayer and supplication on the land. Zechariah declared, "Ask the Lord" (Zech. 10:1a). Many people are crying out in prayer to the Lord today in America. More and more churches have extended prayer meetings two, three, or four hours long. All night prayer meetings are becoming as common as they are in Korea. What an honor to prepare for such services! Roll out some carpet for our soft feeble knees. Obtain recliner chairs for those who are in pain but want to stay and pray. Find quiet worshipful CDs that you can play in the background when needed. You can even hang pictures of prayer points or bring maps of particular regions you wish to pray over during that meeting.

Recently, there was an all-night prayer meeting in Herndon, Virginia. This was part of a prayer and evangelism meeting. I had driven twenty hours to be there at these sessions and was very tired after the first night's agenda. I would gladly have stayed in the all-night prayer meeting, but I needed to lie down and rest my painful back. I had no pillow; I had nothing to rest on. So I went to my guest's home and slept until God woke me up at 4:00 a.m. I went back to the meeting and was able to merge into it, but I felt badly that the facilities had been inadequate for at least two of us who had been waiting on God for a healing.

Pain is not the worst thing in the world. But still we need to do all we can to encourage all who want to come and pray. Therefore, prepare and plan for the weak and those with physical infirmities. I recall having all-night prayer meetings at Prayer Valley. What a tremendous experience we had together. I personally could not have been a part of this prayer meeting if I could not have lain on my back at times on a small office couch we had in our prayer room. At the International House of Prayer in Kansas City, I was happy and surprised to see two special lounge chairs labeled for those who have back problems.

Plan for Positions

Be aware of who is praying with you and their physical conditions. This point is closely tied in with the previous thought. Someone has wisely said, "The mind can only absorb what the seat can endure." This principle applies to prayer meetings. Don't stand too long or hold hands too long. Often older folks and people with physical problems find it very difficult to be in this position for an extended period of time.

We must be aware that because of size or age, some people may have a limited amount of energy and cannot stand long. Recently while holding hands with two older ladies at the end of the prayer meeting, I thought they were both going to pull me down because they were beginning to waiver. It is often too hard to stand still for a long period of time.

There is another position that we must plan for in prayer meetings—kneeling. Paul definitely spent time kneeling in prayer. Twice the book of Acts points out that Paul said goodbye to his friends and knelt down to pray with them:

> I have shewed you all things, how that so labouring ye ought to support the weak, and to remember the words of the Lord Jesus, how he said, It is more blessed to give than to receive. And when he had thus spoken, he kneeled down, and prayed with them all. And they

all wept sore, and fell on Paul's neck, and kissed him, sorrowing most of all for the words which he spake, that they should see his face no more. And they accompanied him unto the ship. (Acts 20:35-38 KJV)

There is a touching verse in Acts 21:5, which gives us this picture as Paul was saying goodbye to his friends at Miletus.

And when we had accomplished those days, we departed and went our way; and they all brought us on our way, with wives and children, till we were out of the city: and we kneeled down on the shore, and prayed. (Acts 21:5 KJV)

They knelt down in the sand and prayed! This is a beautiful picture and an example for Christians in their church prayer meetings. We are often far too familiar with our Almighty God. Our children are flippant because they do not see in the adults the awesome reverence that is due Him. They do not see us kneeling humbly in prayer. Look at the way in which Peter prayed for a woman to be raised up from death:

Then Peter arose and went with them. When he was come, they brought him into the upper chamber: and all the widows stood by him weeping, and shewing the coats and garments which Dorcas made, while she was with them. But Peter put them all forth, and kneeled down, and prayed; and turning him to the body said, Tabitha, arise. And she opened her eyes: and when she saw Peter, she sat up. And he gave her his hand, and lifted her up, and when he had called the saints and widows, presented her alive. (Acts 9:39-41 KJV)

Even our Lord Jesus engaged in kneeling prayer. He knelt when He washed the disciples' feet at the last supper, and He knelt in the Garden of Gethsemane on the night He was arrested, tried, and sentenced to death:

And when he was at the place, he said unto them, Pray that ye enter not into temptation. And he was withdrawn from them about a stone's cast, and kneeled down, and prayed, saying, Father, if thou be willing, remove this cup from me: nevertheless not my will, but thine, be done. (Luke 22:40-42 KJV)

We can see our Lord's contrite and obedient heart as He knelt down to pray to His Father during His last hours here on earth.

Do you see kneeling in prayer at the meetings you attend? I hope so! Thank God for the traditional churches—Catholic, Episcopal, Lutheran—where they have kneeling benches. In many Protestant churches, there are no provisions for kneeling, and some don't even think of kneeling in church. Some, of course, make no provision for kneeling, yet people do often kneel regardless. A powerful prayer meeting will have kneeling people. Kneeling and humility go together. Pastors can roll out carpets in the front area where no carpet is in order to make an altar. If you or someone you know cannot kneel due to a physical problem, don't feel condemned. Simply humble yourself and apply that position within in your heart when you come to pray. God will notice!

I will never forget when Ray Bringham and I were having a renewal day at a Mennonite conference in Pennsylvania. The Holy Spirit told me to plan to start that conference on our knees. I believe I surprised many people when I said, "Here we are in a beautiful church with carpet on the floor. Let us all kneel down and pray as we begin this day."

A missionary came to me later that day and said, "This is what we need on our mission fields, more humble praying."

Three years later, I met a lady who had been at that conference and she said, "You know, I'll never forget how we all knelt down to begin that powerful day of prayer and renewal."

As we plan for different positions in our corporate prayer meetings, let's most of all plan for kneeling. Even more than that, leave room for falling on our faces before our Almighty Holy God.

We need the priority of prayer not only in our churches. We need it in our church conferences, retreats, and missionary journeys. I recently heard a beautiful African brother from the nation of Zaire speak. We were at a week-long conference with the American Baptist Convention at Green Lake, Wisconsin, where there was really very little corporate prayer. This brother spoke out as they were discussing the problem of renewal in the denomination. He told the story, "In our biannual conference in Zaire, the first day is given over to prayer, praise, and testimony." What, a day of prayer to start a conference? Isn't that beautiful!

Practical matters have a lot to do with keeping people away from prayer meetings because we have made it look as though they were not important.

In concluding this chapter on practical principles for powerful prayer meetings, I want to say that I realize that most of these principles have to do with outward things. However, I know, too, that the secret to powerful corporate prayer meetings is the secret prayer closet where the individual Christian meets God alone in prayer. And the prayer meetings will not be more powerful than we are in our secret closets alone with God. At the same time, I know that these practical matters have a lot to do with hindering the flow of prayer in our prayer meetings. These practical matters have a lot to do with keeping people away from prayer meetings because we have made it look as though a person with this need or that need is not important—we didn't prepare for their presence.

The prayer meeting is the closest thing to God's heart in our churches. This is because asking and receiving is God's ordained way to receive power to run the kingdom's work and to get the job done in reaching the lost world for His glory. Without mighty prevailing prayer, God is being robbed from seeing His work accomplished.

It is important that all persons in the church are encouraged to come to prayer meetings. They should know that you are planning for them to come. Help them to understand that as individuals we need to cry out to the Lord in private prayer and in corporate group prayer. It does a soul good psychologically, emotionally, and spiritually to cry out unto the Lord. Why? Because God hears out of His holy hill and answers our prayer.

Corporate Prayer is God's Symphony

God wants to hear each one's voice. God made the voice. Each person's voice is unique and special. Therefore, each prayer is a special prayer. Remember, corporate prayer is God's symphony. We are individually His special instruments. The Holy Spirit is the conductor who brings forth beautiful music for the Master.

I once heard Viterbo University in La Crosse perform Handel's Messiah.

I was in the balcony and observed that the kettle drummer and two horn players did very little through the whole performance. Then the climax came and the Hallelujah Chorus was sung. It was during this last five minutes that these players loudly participated. How very necessary their parts were in this magnificent oratorio. Without the voices of the kettledrums, the symphony would have been ruined. So it is with our voice in corporate prayer meetings.

Another reason why all should be encouraged to pray and lift up voices is that Christians don't realize that their expressed prayer can be used by God to be the very highlight (and high life) for another Christian. Our prayers of faith, thanksgiving, adoration, pleading, and consecration do meet needs in others' lives. These prayers can be teaching prayers. Who knows what great grace is imparted to others through the prayer of each individual? That's why we must spotlight every individual in the sense that we want to encourage all to lift up their voices to pray or participate in some way.

Search My Heart, O God...

1. When I read this chapter, I thought of a few changes I can make in my prayer group. The most important change is

_____

_____

2. Other changes I'd like to consider are:

_____

_____

_____

3. When I read this chapter, an individual person came to mind—someone who may come to our meeting if I provide a place for them to comfortably position themselves while we pray corporately. This person's name is

_____

4. After reading the verses on prayer and kneeling, I have the following thoughts about kneeling in prayer:

_____

_____

_____

_____

Search me, O God, and know my heart: try me, and know my thoughts. (Ps. 139:23)

Chapter 9

GOING DEEPER

THERE ARE NO limits to the exciting varieties of expression and intercession when the Holy Spirit comes. He loves to engage in our prayer! Let's look now at some areas that will take us deeper into the meaning, expressions, and benefits of prayer.

Posting Requests

I have attended thousands of prayer meetings, but I have never seen what was done in Willoughby, Ohio. I entered the church and saw what must have been sixty people crammed into this large room on prayer meeting night. It was an independent Bible church. I knew a person who had attended there for many years, and so I went. What surprised me was that there were so many people at the prayer meeting. But secondly, it was the way the pastor conducted the prayer meeting. He took most of the hour to ask people for their requests, and he laboriously wrote each request on a great big blackboard up front.

After that, we broke up into groups and prayed over the prayer requests, and I suppose we had ten or fifteen minutes to pray. The interesting thing was not only did a lot of people come out for prayer, but a lot of people prayed. Writing their requests on the blackboard evidently gave people a chance to participate not only with their voices to say, "Folks, here's my prayer request," but also the pastor thought it was important to write on the board in front of them all. They prayed for these many requests. You might try this for variety in your prayer meeting.

Prayer without Words

Do you know there are three ways to express prayer?

1. Prayer with words

2. Prayer without words

3. Prayer with other words in the Spirit

I experienced prayer without words in a group meeting one time in Tennessee. We had a group of pastors together in a motel on a retreat/revival meeting. We were preparing for Sunday services, but also we gathered together that we might minister one to another. I had a tremendous backache that day and was in a lot of pain.

Throughout our prayer time, a little, thin man with a beard kept coming up to me and touching my back. In fact, he rubbed my back. He did this several times throughout the evening, but I don't recall him ever praying for my back or for me. Now he may have, but I don't remember that.

What I do remember? I remember that I felt such compassion come from this man—not only that day but also at times after that when I met him. He was so mellow, so quiet in spirit, and just from his very being came this spirit of compassion. I felt better just being in his presence.

I met him again the next day at a large Episcopal church, and lo and behold, he was one of the associate priests there. To my surprise, I found out that he had been divorced twice, and this was his third marriage. I was introduced to his lovely wife. I know the thought went through my mind and my inner being, "How can a twice-divorced man have such compassion and power, the power of Jesus in his life to heal?"

Touched with Jesus's compassion by a prayer said without words

Well, the Lord certainly had to rebuke me and let me know that divorced people can have God's power in prayer also. In fact, they can have more of His power because they themselves have experienced His healing power in prayer. It is really interesting to me to look back on that incident and remember how I was touched with Jesus's compassion by a prayer that was said without words. You and I also can have such power by spending much time in the presence of Jesus.

Honesty in Prayer Brings Victory

In 1980 it was still rare to find preachers of different denominations coming together for prayer. There was such a meeting in Massachusetts. Once a month, preachers gathered together for prayer, and they even fasted their noon meal and continued for a couple of hours in prayer. This was very unusual, and I felt honored to be in Massachusetts at this prayer meeting.

There were over eighty pastors there, and during the course of the well-organized prayer meeting, something unusual happened. I was surprised by the honesty of this pastor's prayer when he prayed, "God, why do I have so many fears in my life? Why do these fears continue to torment me?" And he mentioned other things regarding fear in his life during this prayer.

I thought, *Dear God, what honesty! What total openness!*

Honesty brings deliverance and victory.

One of the key factors to having prayers answered is that we must be brutally honest with God. David was this way!

> Why are you cast down, O my soul? And why are you disquieted within me? Hope in God; for I shall yet praise Him. (Ps. 42:11)

We can see from his writing here, that David was very honest and open. Many times we do not have our prayers answered because we do not become honest with God and our Christian friends who could pray with us and give us comfort and instruction.

David, at the end of Psalm 42, found the victory. In fact, in the middle of his discouragement he said,

> The Lord will command His lovingkindness in the daytime, and in the night His song shall be with me—a prayer to the God of my life. (Ps. 42:8)

Honesty brings deliverance and victory!

One Way to Get Silence

Silence can be golden. One of the most abused aspects of a prayer meeting is that we do not become quiet when the Lord tells us to be quiet, and we feel that we must keep on saying words. I was in a 5:00 a.m. prayer meeting at an Episcopal church in Tennessee. Each morning the prayer meeting ended with a beautiful celebration of Communion. In this prayer meeting, there certainly were some seasoned prayer warriors.

One thing that was different in this prayer meeting was that it was organized and liturgical. By that I mean the priest had an order that he went through and read out of his prayer book according to the religious calendar of the year. There were scriptures bringing a theme on each one of the five mornings I was there. There was a time for intercessory prayer. And my, how those people prayed! The interesting thing was that God, by His spirit, was calling for a time of silence. The person next to me started praying, and it was obvious that it was out of place. A very unique thing happened that taught me a lesson I pass on to you.

---

*Singing a chorus is a good way to bring
focus to a prayer group.*

I always wondered how to get silence in a prayer meeting when the Holy Spirit is calling for silence and people will not be quiet. The whole group began to very softly sing the chorus, "Be Still and Know that I am God." We all got the message, and there was a time of quietness. I was impressed by a music teacher who recently said, "In music, we need to have a silent pause to be able to appreciate the next score." One time God said, "You have wearied the Lord with your words" (Mal. 2:17a). Singing a chorus is a good way to bring focus to a prayer group.

Let's all pray that we will learn to flow with the Holy Spirit and not rob God of our holy awe and worship. When the time comes for silence and waiting on God, we will not feel uncomfortable. We will all feel very comfortable in His great presence and in holy silence.

Is Your Prayer Meeting a Secret?

Prayer meetings seem to be some of the best kept secrets of churches, conferences, and retreat centers. This should not be. I often have to ask, "Do you have a prayer meeting here?" In fact, that happened this very week. A meeting had not been advertised, but because I asked I was able to enjoy some good prayer time.

This was also true in a retreat center that I visited. I had been to a couple of their evening meetings and had literature in my hand. But I could not find one word about the early morning prayer meeting they were having each morning at 6:00 a.m. It was not announced from the pulpit with the many other announcements that were given. Nobody on the platform seemed to be excited about the early prayer meeting. They seemed excited about all the guest speakers coming in the next ten days but not about prayer.

I went to the early morning prayer meeting, and as usual there was no one there to greet me or tell me what was going on. After all, it was "only" a prayer meeting. You were supposed to enter and do your own thing. I went into the sanctuary and knelt, and I appreciated the quietness.

All of a sudden, from out of the side room, somebody shouted, "Praise the Lord!" I was startled, but I began to praise the Lord anyway. Three days later, I learned their system. After about a half hour of silent prayer alone with God, they would begin to praise the Lord. After praise they would enter into intercessory prayer requests and then end by holding hands and praying in a circle. Glory to God! There was power at that prayer meeting. There was a flow of the Holy Spirit. There was fervency, and there were tears of anguish for souls.

However, how nice it would have been to be informed concerning the procedures instead of having to feel my way through the service. A bulletin or opening statement would solve this awkwardness.

Wednesday morning was different. At the very beginning of the prayer meeting, a man came to the pulpit dressed in a suit and led the meeting. It was obvious after a while that he was a preacher and was to share a word. There was no flow of the Holy Spirit in that prayer meeting for the rest of that morning.

I was aware that in our midst there were two great piano players. I thought, "What a shame that one of these pianists was not used to bring glory to God in this prayer meeting by leading us in worship."

It was obvious that the preacher was unprepared to lead this prayer meeting, and it was a difficult prayer meeting to endure.

Unprepared preachers make prayer meetings difficult to endure.

May God help us to stop treating our prayer meetings as being only for the "old timers" or "regulars." Let us publicize them well, expect strong attendance, and be excited about our prayer meetings. And above all, let's use our best talents in our prayer meetings! Let's offer our Lord the best music, scripture reading, and praise.

Do Tongues Disturb You?

The misuse of speaking or praying in tongues often brings confusion and anxiety in group prayer meetings. I was in a Baptist church in Wilmington, Delaware, on a Wednesday night. We had our choice of doing several options, one of which was a prayer meeting. I chose the prayer meeting.

Monopolizing a prayer meeting in any way is not wise.

There were approximately thirty people in that room sitting in a circle. They had a chair in the middle for those who asked for specific prayers. Each time somebody sat in the chair for prayer, this one brother would lay hands on him and pray loudly in tongues. However, there was no interpretation of the tongues, and we wondered what he was praying. This did not happen just once, but several times in that forty-five minutes of prayer. This dear brother monopolized that prayer meeting with his constant praying loudly and boldly in tongues.

Monopolizing a prayer meeting in any way is not wise. I am sure he thought he was doing well praying over people and issues, but I was very disturbed because I could not participate with understanding. I was frustrated because I felt a violation of biblical principles. Paul wrote in First Corinthians chapter fourteen that, if there are tongues given, either that person praying in tongues or someone in the group should give an interpretation in the normal language so everyone can understand what the Spirit of God is saying and praying. And there were no interpretations.

To say the least, there was anxiety and confusion, and only God knows how much good came forth from that prayer meeting. Let's look at what Paul wrote about speaking in tongues:

> I thank my God I speak with tongues more than you all; yet in the church I would rather speak five words with my understanding, that I may teach others also, than ten thousand words in a tongue. (1 Cor. 14:18-19)

This was a problem the Corinthian church had, and it is a problem the Church still has today in some of its prayer meetings. It is marvelous to be zealous for the Lord, but we must be discerning and not push praying in tongues on others.

Prayer is not a Shouting Match

I couldn't believe my ears as to what was happening in this prayer meeting in Northern California. There were about thirty of us in this room when a dear sister was called upon to lead in a prayer. She took the microphone and began to pray. Before I knew it, everybody else was praying out loud at the top of his or her voice. Even though this dear sister had a microphone, I could not hear what she was praying. This went on for a few minutes and finally the amens were said. I sat there a little bit puzzled. I could not hear what the sister had prayed, so I could not say amen to her prayer.

Everybody else must have known by reading her mind because they certainly couldn't hear her voice. Here again I believe we had confusion in the prayer meeting. The next day I told the people how I felt—that I could not enter into the prayer, that I felt embarrassed and left out, and that if they called on me to lead prayer, I would appreciate it if they would not all shout me down.

Certainly there are times when I believe this kind of praying is appropriate. For example, when a topic is announced such as praying for our government leaders, someone may lead off by announcing, "We are now going to pray for the President, Vice-President, his cabinet, their wives, and their families." Then we would begin to pray all together in unison. I see nothing wrong with this because I have been in those situations, and we all know what we are praying about. I believe in these cases that we are praying with one accord and with one heart, and God hears and is pleased with the many voices.

There is something to be said about this type of praying in that even the most timid will often cry out from their hearts to God for the petitions in the midst of what others might say is noise. However, to ask someone to lead in prayer without a specific topic or request and then to shout your prayers louder than the leaders seems to be very out of place and inappropriate.

There is a Bible illustration in Acts chapter four where the multitude lifted up their voices with one accord. It gives the impression that everybody prayed out loud. This prayer was recorded by the Holy Spirit in the Holy Scriptures so we must assume that the prayer was heard and understood. We have the beautiful results there of praying together in one accord and even lifting our voices together over a certain issue.

That prayer meeting evolved when Peter and James were first persecuted and were commanded to no longer preach in Jesus's name. The prayer meeting resulted in more preaching with signs, wonders, and more people getting saved. Glory!

Have you ever been to a prayer meeting where there were three to five thousand people praying?

Have you ever been to a prayer meeting where there were three to five thousand people praying? Until recently in America, we have not had such prayer meetings. However, now we find there are some concerts of prayer that are drawing this many people to pray in a very wonderful, structured way. However, for years they have been praying in multitudes of numbers like this in South Korea.

An All-night Prayer Meeting

I remember my first experience of being in an all-night prayer meeting in Korea. I don't know how many thousands of people were there. They not only filled the gymnasium but also filled the outside courtyards. I remember going to try to find some water, and I passed another building where I could hear the noise of hundreds of people praying together. Well, you've guessed it. This was at Dr. Cho's church in South Korea.

You might be interested to know how a prayer meeting with thousands is manageable. First, I want to report that the meeting was orderly and was led by the pastor who utilized a bell. There was a message from the Word of God.

There was a time for people to come forward to give testimonies and to be healed. There were several occasions where topics were announced for prayer. Everybody raised their voices in unison to God and began to pray. I assure you the joyful noise could be heard for blocks. It sounded like a great rally in a football field. How exciting it was to hear these thousands of people praying.

The meeting was orderly and led by a pastor who utilized a bell.

When the pastor wanted to go on to another subject or phase of the prayer meeting, he rang a bell. They would stop praying, and sometimes they would sing a hymn. We might wonder how these people could work all day (many I'm told up to sixteen hours) and pray all night. How could mothers be there with their babies? They simply laid their babies on the floor, or tied them on their backs, and the babies slept. Many people were obviously tired and would catch naps in between some of the praying. How amazing it is that for years this kind of praying has gone on in South Korea.

I'm told that there is a Presbyterian church that has three successive hour-long prayer meetings starting at 4:00, 5:00, and 6:00 a.m. You have to be there early to get into the prayer meeting you want because so many attend. People come in the front door, and when the place is full, they shut the door. After the one hour is up, they are ushered out the back door as newcomers flow through the front door.

If you are in South Korea from 4:00 a.m. to 7:00 a.m., you will get in a traffic jam. It's not only people hurrying to work. It's people rushing to prayer meetings. This is what the Spirit of God is doing.

There are some extenuating circumstances that help Korea to be such a praying nation. Forty miles or less from Dr. Cho's church you can see the border where North Korean communists have their guns aimed upon South Korea. Nevertheless, this church, which is one of the largest in the world, is certainly a church that is built upon the priority of prayer. There is no doubt that all nations are saying that the church in South Korea is a house of prayer.

I might add that I have never seen more fervency in prayer and more energy expended as when they prayed. They seemed to be shaking their fists at Satan. Ladies and men were on their haunches rocking back and forth as they prayed and being very violent with their hand movements. You would have thought they were in a boxing match. Certainly they were in a boxing match with the evil powers as they were crying out to God for the deliverance of many precious souls that were in darkness. The Koreans know the reality of these scriptures:

> For we do not wrestle against flesh and blood, but against principalities, against powers, against the rulers of the darkness of this age, against spiritual hosts of wickedness in the heavenly places. (Eph. 6:12)

> For the weapons of our warfare are not carnal but mighty in God for pulling down strongholds. (2 Cor. 10:4)

> And from the days of John the Baptist until now the kingdom of heaven suffers violence, and the violent take it by force. (Matt. 11:12)

> So shall they fear the name of the Lord from the west, and His glory from the rising of the sun; When the enemy comes in like a flood, the Spirit of the Lord will lift up a standard against him. (Isa. 59:19)

Here is a church in South Korea moving forward by the supernatural power of the priority of prayer. We pray in Jesus's name that this will also soon be so in America. Let the intercessors in America pray with the same scriptural understanding and the same fervency!

After I was in Korea, I was in a prayer rally with sixteen thousand in San Francisco's Candlestick Park Stadium where the fervency was nearly equal to Korea. Can this be a forerunner sign of revival?

Distractions

Outside Vista, California (near San Diego), we met for a pastors/leaders prayer meeting one day in a Catholic monastery. I came back the next day to be alone with God. I was put into a beautiful little room where I had many hours of wonderful quietness with God.

---

*Be careful not to be a temptation to others
by the way we dress.*

I came out to walk around and stretch my legs and was I ever shocked. I looked and I couldn't believe what I saw walking toward me. It was a beautiful woman in black tight pants. Needless to say, my mind was not on prayer very long. Not only were her pants as tight as they could be, but she had a lot to show off. I thought, *God, is this for real or is this the Devil? What is she doing here in a monastery?*

I believe I did talk to her, but I hastened back to my private room thinking, *Wow, it does make a difference how ladies dress when at a prayer meeting.* So ladies and men both, let us be careful that we are not a temptation to others due to the way we dress. Let us be modest in our dress so that we glorify God in our attire and our prayers.

Communion and Prayer

The Holy Spirit taught me a very important lesson in Wichita, Kansas. Holy Communion and prayer go together beautifully in prayer meetings. A unique feature of this prayer meeting was that it was well planned, held in a lovely chapel, and an organist was playing some older familiar hymns in a skillful manner.

I have been to hundreds of early morning prayer meetings, and usually they show little or no planning. Please don't get me wrong, because we really cannot plan our praying in a prayer meeting, but we can give some thought to the music and prayer topics. We can give some thought to the purpose of what God wants in that prayer meeting. We can arrange the chairs, and we can be prepared to begin with. There needs to be some planning and some praying for every prayer meeting. We certainly do not want to plan God out of the service. We want to be open to the moving of the Holy Spirit in the praying.

This prayer meeting was planned, and it made such a difference for those attending. One new and interesting part of this meeting was that the communion elements were prepared at the altar for those who wanted to partake of Holy Communion. There was a time for quietness and a time for group petition, and prayer cards were handed out with requests that came in from the morning services. No wonder there were so many people there at the 6:00 a.m. prayer meeting to try and meet the Lord!

The keys to church growth are found in Acts 2:42. Here we find they continued steadfastly in the apostles' doctrine, in fellowship, in breaking of bread, and in prayers.

Holy Communion and praying go together.

In most Protestant churches, there is not enough time for Holy Communion and prayer. Holy Communion and praying go together. Catholic and many Episcopalian Christians have opportunity every day to partake of the Lord's Supper. Most Protestant churches squeeze in the Lord's Holy Communion once a month. When we look at the cross, we are always lifted up and strengthened, infused with His love and power, and challenged to be obedient servants. We find strength to obey all our Lord's words and the challenge to make His Church a house of prayer.

It is very important for me to tell you that this communion service was done in simplicity. The elements were put at the altar. People knew that they were there, and they could come and kneel at the altar to partake and wait on the Lord.

Oh, how we need altars in our churches. If you don't have one, make a simple one. Roll out a piece of carpet by some chairs, and invite people to kneel in prayer as they partake of Holy Communion. Even during the prayer times, I believe kneeling will put some fire back into the prayer meetings.

This Church of God is one of the fastest growing churches in America, especially since they have made prayer a priority in their program. Yes, they do have a prayer coordinator. It doesn't matter what we call these individuals, but somebody needs to have the responsibility to work with the pastor and to see that prayer opportunities are planned. A plan will give opportunity to the church to obey the new command of the Lord to come together and to ask for whatever we need in His name.

What Happened to the Pastoral Prayer?

In a town near Murfreesboro, Tennessee, a Presbyterian pastor amazed our prayer team in the morning service. He began to pray a very impassioned prayer for his sheep. He came from behind the pulpit and walked down the aisles, putting his hands over the people. The pastor prayed while walking up and down the long aisles in the church. He must have prayed five to eight minutes over his sheep.

How wonderful, I thought. *Here is a church that knows how much their pastor cares as he prays over his sheep with great sincerity and earnestness.*

I go to many churches and find that the pastors do not offer what we used to call the pastoral prayer. In fact, they usually ask me to lead in prayer. I think, *Pastor, you are missing a great opportunity to publicly pray for your sheep and show them that you care as a pastor.* I gladly pray. I search the bulletin to find out who is sick and what needs may be mentioned. I feel most honored when I am asked to lead a congregation in prayer.

When I was a young Christian in Cleveland, Ohio, I used to drive children back and forth from church. I hurried to take the children home because I was so eager to hear my pastor pray. I didn't want to miss the pastor's prayer over the congregation. I remember one instance when I got a ticket for speeding. I arrived at the church and quickly hurried in just in time to stand at the back door to listen to Pastor Edwin Miller leading the sheep in prayer. Now isn't it amazing that I wanted to hear him pray as much as I wanted to hear him preach? I was blessed by the pastor's prayer.

Ray Bringham, a prayer evangelist, told me a story about when he was in England with his family. They were in this great historic church when the pastor led the congregation in the pastoral prayer.

"It was a long prayer," Ray said. "Almost fifteen minutes until the pastor was done."

His sixteen-year-old son turned to him and said, "Dad, I feel like I have been fed. We can go home now."

Beloved, we just cannot imagine the ministry of the Holy Spirit through the prayers that come from a pastor's heart for his sheep.

Pastors, don't let prayer die! Use this opportunity to make your church a house of prayer as your sheep catch the vision and the burden for prayer from your heart.

Music with Prayer

Music is one of God's most powerful gifts to man. We can use both singing and instruments, together or separate, in our prayer times in special ways.

Perhaps you've heard the old saying; "He can make that musical instrument talk." That saying applies to our prayer times! Some are gifted to prophecy through playing of music.

Joann came to visit us at Prayer Valley especially to pray for us. She sat at the piano and began to play. We began to sing, and before you know it, after each song, we began to offer praise and petition. This went on for over an hour. As we prayed, waited and sang, and listened to the various songs, the ministry of music came from this sister playing the piano. I can only say it was one of the most unusual times of prayer I have ever had.

I heard about a church in Kansas City that had prayer meetings every morning in different parts of that city. I was there and since the day was a holiday, I doubted if a prayer meeting would be held. I asked a brother who attended there if they would be having the prayer meeting.

Very excitedly he said, "Oh, we never miss; we pray every morning of the year." So they had a real steadfast spirit about prayer.

The next morning, my son-in-law, Mark, and I drove across the city, and approximately an hour later we arrived at this prayer meeting after six thirty in the morning. The unusual feature about this meeting was that instead of it going an hour and a half, it lasted almost three hours.

The use of music was very different. When they began to pray, there was someone at the piano, the drums, and the organ. They played music all through the prayer times, and they would get louder and they would get softer. They would stop for a moment or two, but for the most part they kept playing. It enhanced the meeting for a while, but I want to emphasize that too much of the same rhythm and too much of the same beat can become distracting.

Use music discreetly in your prayer meetings, but do use it. Remember the psalms were sung, and they were prayed. You can have an exciting prayer meeting with your musical instruments.

Saul had his problems; he was troubled by evil spirits. Nothing seemed to help the great king until he called David with his harp to play for him. Saul knew who to call for help—a man of music and prayer!

As Christians, we can say that our success is indeed in whom we know. When we go to prayer, we learn to wield the mighty weapon of prayer in Jesus's name. I believe the world and the backslider will more and more call upon the church to pray for them in their dire needs. For truly the answer to life's problems are in our heavenly King Jesus.

A wonderful way to evangelize our communities is to go to the neighbors and share that the church cares. Ask them if they have problems the church can pray for. Share the several prayer programs of the church when prayers are offered. Also tell them the church is open for their personal prayers morning, noon, and night. Someone could be there to have personal altar prayer with them. Oh, that our churches might be known as houses of prayer, solving human crises with humbling cries of prayer.

Search My Heart, O God...

1. Which scriptures would I like a pastor to pray over me? Write them here:

_____

_____

_____

_____

2. Write down a pastoral prayer (from the Holy Spirit's leading) that I can pray over the people who attend the prayer service that I lead:

_____

_____

_____

_____

3. Do I like to include music when I pray alone in my prayer closet? _____
What are my favorite songs, CDs, or instruments to utilize during private prayer?

_____

_____

_____

_____

4. What helps me to go deeper in prayer? What enhances my prayer time more than anything else? Can this be incorporated into prayers in a large group setting?

_____

_____

_____

_____

_____

_____

_____

_____

Search me, O God, and know my heart: try me, and know my thoughts. (Ps. 139:23)

Chapter 10

THE SECRET OF PERSEVERING PRAYER

THE GREATEST REASON for persevering in prayer is that Jesus said to persevere.

How can I give up on others when I know that a merciful God never gives up on me?

It's so exciting to hear somebody praying who won't give up! How exciting it is to meet champions in life who refuse to quit! Perseverance is a quality that we all admire, whether it is in athletics, business, or any endeavor.

There is a woman in Scripture of that character. You read about her in Matthew chapter fifteen and in Mark chapter seven. She was called a woman of Canaan, a Syrophenician woman. She was looked down upon by the Jewish community because she was a pagan, yet she had a great need—her daughter was demon possessed. Who could help her in her dilemma? Who could help her in her hurts? Who could help her in this pain of life?

She had heard that there was a Jesus of Nazareth, who was helping people. He was coming to her community. Actually, Mark says, "And He entered a house and wanted no one to know it" (Mark 7:24).

But she found Him; she sought Him out. She had hope that He would heal her daughter. But instead of answering her prayer cry, He discouraged her. We find this story to be a picture of you and me. With roadblocks to answers to prayer that discourage us, we can be tempted to shut down and quit asking.

A Secret about God

When Jesus spoke the Sermon on the Mount and gave a teaching about prayer, He taught the people to keep on asking, seeking, and knocking. In that very first sermon, He indicated the secret of this persevering type of prayer.

"If you then, being evil, know how to give good gifts to your children, how much more will your Father who is in heaven give good things to those who ask Him!" (Matt. 7:11)

Yes, the indication of a secret is found in those words, "How much more will your Father give..."

The secret is in knowing the character of our God to whom we pray. I would like to call Him a "much more" God which is our God of abundant giving. The Syrophenician woman came to Jesus seeking help in a desperate situation. No doubt she had gone to many other places for help, and they could not help her. It's like the world that we live in today. It is getting more and more burdened down with the results of sin and death and the complicated relationships. It seems like there is no hope. But the scriptures tell us He is a God of hope (Romans 15:13). This woman went to Jesus. Being discouraged, she had every reason to stop asking and turn away from Him.

Three Road Blocks to Answers

We find roadblocks in answers to the Syrophenician woman's prayers in three ways.

The Silence of God

The first roadblock is the silence of God. Jesus would not answer her a single word. How often we get discouraged over the silence of God when we ceaselessly pray. It seems as though nothing is happening. That's where perseverance needs to come forth more and more in simply believing that God is a God who hears and answers prayer. Don't get angry at God for His silent delays.

Unkind Disciples

The second roadblock was the unkind disciples. When the woman could not get one word out of Jesus, she may have thought, *Well, He's tired. He doesn't want to be bothered, so I will go to His disciples. I've heard that they also have authority and power to cast out demons and to heal the sick.* Scripture says she asked the disciples, and the disciples came to Jesus saying, "Send her away, for she cries out after us" (Matt. 15:23b). They didn't want anything to do with this pagan woman. Well, can you see how she might have been discouraged?

Today we still see many times when Jesus's disciples hurt each other with some of these same words. This carelessness of Christians is one of those "ought not to be so" cautions in the Bible. Too often careless words of one can make another want to give up and say, "Well, if this is what Christianity is, then I don't want any part of it!"

In our struggle to "keep on keeping on," the Holy Spirit gently reminds us that we are to look unto Jesus, the "author and finisher of our faith" (Heb. 12:2). We are not to look to the disciples (who can let us down), or to other men and women who are sinners just like we are. Many times they have hurt us. These disciples were maybe more discouraging than Jesus.

Jesus wouldn't answer the Syrophenician woman a word. They probably said, "Go away woman. We want nothing to do with you." That's indicated because they went to Jesus and said, "She's troubling us. Send her away."

But she wouldn't give up! She came to Jesus again, and we read that she said a second time, "Lord, help me." A real short prayer, isn't it?

Stark-Naked Truth

The third and biggest roadblock is the stark-naked truth. In Matthew 15:26 we read finally that Jesus answered, but He insults her by saying, "It is not good to take the children's bread and throw it to the little dogs." And so she was insulted. But that didn't stop her.

She openly stood before Him and said, "Yes, Lord, yet even the little dogs eat the crumbs which fall from their masters' table" (Matt. 15:27). In other words, "The truth of the matter is, you're right. I am a pagan; I'm not a Jew. I have no right to come to you, the Messiah, who came first to the Jew."

The woman said, "It's *true* that my daughter has a demon that no one can seem to cast out. It's *true* that I am a Gentile. It's *true* that I am called a dog by society. But I won't give up!"

In our life's situations, we also feel it's true that the person I'm praying for seems like the most improbable person to be born again. It's *true* that this cancer my loved one has seems to be fatal. It's *true* that my son or daughter who has been away from the Lord so long has become so hardened that it doesn't seem as though he or she could ever come back to the Lord. It's true that my marriage is not good, and I see it day after day more likely heading for the divorce court. It's true I don't have the money I need to pay my bill. It's true, Lord, I have all these problems.

Yes, the truth of the matter seems to overwhelm us. It seems like the mountain is too big, but the Lord said, "Men always ought to pray and not lose heart" (Luke 18:1). Keep on praying and don't give up, for nothing is impossible with God! Persevere! An answer will come!

Needed Strength Comes from Obedience

Jesus taught more about persevering in prayer than perhaps any other subject except faith. Jesus told the parable of the widow who went to the unjust judge to ask for justice. She kept on asking and knocking on the door until she got an answer to her request.

When the disciples asked Him, "Lord, teach us to pray," in Luke 11:1, He gave them the eloquent words of The Lord's Prayer, as we know it.

Then He told them a story about a man who had friends visiting him at midnight and how he had no bread to give them. So he went to his neighbor friend and knocked on his door.

The friend responded, "It's midnight! I can't get up and disturb my children by getting up and giving you bread!"

But the man kept on knocking persistently, saying, "You've got to get up. I must be hospitable and give bread to my friends!"

Lack of hospitality in the nations of the Middle East is considered to be a great affront against a person who visits you. Scripture goes on to say, "Yet because of his persistence he will rise and give him as many as he needs" (Luke 11:8). So once again, persistent, persevering prayer got the job done!

Her Secret Revealed

What was the secret that kept this Syrophenician, Canaanite woman pleading with the Lord though He would not answer her a word? She pleaded with the disciples who scorned her. She came to Jesus, again facing the truth of the matter. What kept her going? What great secret made her say, "Lord. I know you should not take children's food and feed it to dogs. However, I am not one of those street dogs that you are talking about, Lord. I'm one of the house dogs; a pet. I'm one of those pets who gets to eat the crumbs that fall from the master's table. You see, Lord, I am of the household of faith, and I just need one crumb of Your mercy, Your love, Your power to help me."

"Then Jesus answered and said to her, 'O woman, great is your faith! Let it be to you as you desire.' And her daughter was healed from that very hour" (Matt. 15:28).

The key or secret to persevering prayer is knowing the mercy of God.

What was the secret? Ah, the secret of persevering prayer is found in the second word of this woman's mouth as she came to Jesus. She knelt before Him and said, "Have mercy on me, O Lord!" She knew that Jesus was a merciful person. That is the key or secret to persevering prayer—knowing the character of God.

Perhaps this pagan woman had heard of the incident in Luke 18:35-43 where Jesus went into a city and a blind man cried out, "Jesus, have mercy on me," but the crowd said, "Be quiet!"

However, the blind man persisted and cried out again, "Jesus, have mercy on me." Jesus said, "Bring him to me." Jesus continued, "What do you want Me to do for you?" (v. 40).

And he said, "Lord, that I may receive my sight."

And Jesus touched him and he was healed. I don't know how this woman knew that Jesus was such a merciful man except that the testimony of His character must have followed Him all through the land.

What is Mercy

The older I get the more I realize we need mercy. My simple definition of mercy is "help for the helpless." It is those who are helpless who find help from a merciful Savior.

"Mercy," someone said, "is getting more than we deserve." We usually identify mercy with sin, but uses a broader reference as well. The word *mercy* involves the easing of pain, the holding back of a penalty. It also points to obtaining comfort and help from pain at death.

Surely goodness and mercy shall follow me all the days of my life. (Ps. 23:6)

Yea, though I walk through the valley of the shadow of death, I will fear no evil. (Ps. 23:4)

Webster defines *mercy* as "a deep and tender feeling of compassion aroused by the sight of weakness or suffering to those who are dear to us or need help." Yes, mercy has to do with compassion. Mercy encompasses help extended to others and help received.

His mercy endures forever. (Ezra 3:11)

Remember me, O my God, concerning this also, and spare me according to the greatness of Your mercy! (Neh. 13:22)

In Nehemiah 9:19 God's mercies are manifold. His mercies are marked by diversity and variety. No matter what my need is, if God's mercies are manifold, surely there is enough to meet my needs! No wonder Paul says in 2 Corinthians 1:3 that God is "the Father of mercies."

And so, this woman knew Jesus was a merciful person. It seems to me that He wasn't very kind. He was discouraging her and testing her faith. Nevertheless, she wouldn't give up. She persisted; she persevered. Faith always wins. Her faith in the power of just one little crumb of God's mercy was enough to meet her need.

The psalmist says that God's mercy is characterized by tenderness. Isn't that beautiful?

...Who crowns you with lovingkindness and tender mercies. (Ps. 103:4b)

Turn to me according to the multitude of Your tender mercies. (Ps. 69:16b)

God's merciful ways indeed are ways of tender mercies. God deals with us gently like a mother deals with her little baby. God's people are surrounded by

His mercy, protected from behind by His mercy. Mercy even cleans up many past mistakes. I love this verse:

> Surely goodness and mercy shall follow me all the days of my life...
> (Ps. 23:6a)

Once I shared this verse with a man whose son had just committed suicide, and he was so comforted. Regardless of all the guilt feelings and questions that can overwhelm one at a time like this, the father took great comfort from God's "goodness and mercy." He recognized that this godly mercy and goodness somehow come behind us and clean up our mistakes or messes. God's mercy forgives us and helps us to overcome.

Oh, how great is God's mercy! No wonder the psalmist sang:

> "I will sing aloud of Your mercy in the morning!" (Ps. 59:16)

> "I will sing of the mercies of the Lord forever!" (Ps. 89:1 KJV)

> "They are new every morning: great is thy faithfulness." (Lam. 3:22-23 KJV)

Why should this understanding of His mercy give us such stamina in persevering prayer? Because no matter what our needs are or what we're praying for, God's mercy is able and longing to come to the rescue. It's just that God's timing is not our timing as we think of time. We must wait on the Lord and be of good courage and let Him strengthen our hearts (Ps. 27:14).

Mercy—God Hurting, God Helping, God Giving Hope

Dr. Karl Barth, a well-known theologian, said this about mercy: "The mercy of God lies in His readiness to share in the sympathy to share in the distress of another; a readiness which springs from His innermost nature and stamps all God's being and doing."[15]

You see, God is hurting. Dr. Barth goes on to say, "Mercy lies therefore in God's will. It springs from the depths of His nature and characteristics. God takes the initiative for the removal of this distress."

God begins to help us because He shares in our hurts. This quotation from

Dr. Barth addresses the fact that God participates in our distress, and *sympathy* implies that He is really present in the midst. This means that He wills that it should not be, and that He therefore wills to remove it. Here is where we see that God gives us hope. When we know God is hurting with us and longing to help us, this gives us hope.

The root Hebrew word for *mercy* comes from the same root word which means "a woman's womb." So when Webster defines *mercy* as "a deep and tender feeling of compassion aroused by a sight of weakness or suffering," one has a better grasp of God's pain and tenderness over our distresses. I believe the Syrophenician woman felt that if the testimony of Jesus was that He had helped others, why wouldn't He help her? Wasn't He the Messiah, the God of Israel? So again, don't give up early!

Mercy's Awesome Strengths

Another characterization of the mercy of God is *abundance*. He is always ready to give us so much more than what we can either ask or think! This is so beautiful about the character of God. The word *abundant* means "superfluity, extra, exceedingly abounding." Peter uses this word when he says "Blessed be the God and Father of our Lord Jesus Christ, who according to His *abundant* mercy has begotten us again to a living hope through the resurrection of Jesus Christ from the dead" (1 Pet. 1:3, emphasis added).

This living, wonderful hope lies in a merciful God who is *abundant* in mercy. He is a God full of tender mercies, whose mercies endure forever (Ps. 118:1). His mercies are everlasting and plenteous (Ps. 86:5), who remembers mercy in wrath (Hab. 3:2), and whose mercies are manifold. It is this kind of God we pray to and who said to us:

Call to Me, and I will answer you, and show you great and mighty things, which you do not know. (Jer. 33:3)

Not to turn coward (faint, lose heart, and give up). (Luke 18:1 amp)

And shall God not avenge His own elect who cry out day and night to Him, though He bears long with them? I tell you that He will avenge them speedily. Nevertheless, when the Son of Man comes, will He really find faith on the earth? (Luke 18:7-8)

He can hardly wait to answer your prayers. When all is ready, He will answer.

Worship Gives Unbelievable Strength

There is another secret. A spin-off of knowing that Jesus was merciful kept this woman battling and pressing through. It was the truth of worship. She wouldn't stop worshipping God in the midst of her pain and darkness. She cried out in Matthew 15:25, "Have mercy on me, Oh Lord!"

And even in the midst of the disciples' retort to her, she came back to Jesus and again cried, "Lord, help me." She called Him "Lord" again. She worshipped Him.

When Jesus seemingly discouraged her by insulting her, she still called Him "Lord." "It's true, Lord," she said. She started out kneeling before Him, constantly pleading with Him as Lord, worshipping Him as Lord, and believing in Him as Lord—a merciful Lord.

Biblical Perseverance

The greatest reason for persevering in prayer is that Jesus said to persevere. I am so glad we have many illustrations of persevering in. I am so glad that Abraham persevered in prayer six times for God to hold back His judgment on Sodom and Gomorrah so that his nephew Lot and family could get out of Sodom. I am so glad that Elijah prayed three times over a dead boy. He didn't stop the second time, but he prayed three times in 1 Kings 17:21, and the boy came alive. I'm so glad that Elijah prayed seven times for rain, telling his servant to go each time to see if there were any clouds in the sky.

After the first time, no; second time, no; third time, no; fourth time, no; fifth time, no; and sixth time, no. The seventh time the servant came back and said, "Yes, there is a little cloud the size of a man's hand."

And Elijah said, "That's it."

Naaman, the leper, was glad he persevered and obeyed the command of Elijah to dip seven times. Not one time, not two times, not four times, but seven times to dip in the river. I am so glad for that blind man in Luke 18:35-39 when he cried, "So much the more!" Beloved, that's persevering in prayer. You and I must keep crying, "So much the more! Lord have mercy on me, on my loved ones, on our nation." Keep on persevering, and you will see "little clouds!" Keep on until the rain falls! Until the full answer comes! Remember, our merciful God hurts with us. He will surely come and help us. Therefore, we will have hope while we are praying.

The Prayer of Importunity

I want to share something I've learned about the prayer of importunity.

I shared the story earlier that Jesus told of the man who had unexpected company to come to see him one night. This man went to his neighbor's house and knocked and knocked on the door, even though it was late at night. He shouted, "I have unexpected company! Please, give me some bread to share with them!"

It was an insult in those days not to feed your guests when they visited. The Lord told everyone, "I say unto you, though he will not rise and give him, because he is his friend, yet because of his *importunity* he will rise and give him as many as he needeth" (Luke 11:8, emphasis added).

This is the only time that the word *importunity* is used in the New Testament. The prayer of importunity means unashamedly pleading for a need. David danced unashamedly. When his wife rebuked him for making a fool of himself dancing so openly, David retorted, "What? I will be even more undignified than this!"

The prayer of importunity involves pleading, weeping, bare-faced, crying out unashamedly for a need that is rocking your heart and your world. "The prayer of importunity brings answers that are available in no other way. It has often been said that nothing is beyond the scope of prayer unless it is beyond the will of God. Bold importunity succeeds where all other pleas and prayers fail. Importunity conquers impossible circumstances, drives back overwhelming forces of darkness, and overcomes a seemingly endless succession of hindrances. Importunity binds God to His promises, brings heaven's angels to your assistance, and scatters the demons from hell. Importunity brings God's will into realization when all else fails."[16]

My Uncle Sam understood the prayer of importunity. Unfortunately, my Uncle Sam died and I didn't even know it at the time. I didn't get to go to his funeral. He wasn't living when Dad died, but Uncle Sam prayed for many years. Imagine being slapped for telling a loved one they need Jesus. Would you come back and tell them again? Uncle Sam did. He used to preach to my dad. He was a bachelor and sometimes he'd come and get my sister or me to go with him to church. He'd give us money or a gift.

He was a man of love who knew how to pray for his family.

I prayed for my father, too, for seventeen years. I shared earlier how I actually broke down and wept when I was in seminary. I prayed with tears and importunity. It felt a little uncomfortable doing that, but my burden for my father was so great.

What kept me going during the long wait for his conversion was God's promise and God's mercy. I knew that He was merciful. I knew that if He could transform a Saul to a Paul, He could save my daddy. I wouldn't give up for the mercy of the Lord endures forever. I knew God would answer my prayer of importunity.

The next time you feel like quitting, remember the merciful Savior who would not deny a pagan woman a crumb of His mercy when she persevered in worship and prayer and would not give up. Importunity will win the battle!

The Best Illustration

There is an illustration of perseverance that tops them all. I believe it is Jesus himself in the Garden of Gethsemane when He also experienced the silence of God—even His own Father. He also experienced the failures of His own disciples. Call it a sin if you believe prayerlessness is sin. They fell asleep even though Jesus needed them so desperately to pray with Him. He also faced the awful truth of the matter. He had to become the sin offering.

He had to become the Lamb of God. He had to pour out His blood. So Jesus persevered and prayed, "Father, not My will but Thy will be done." He had to pray three times, probably an hour each time in this struggling prayer. Finally, the victory was won, and He woke up the sleeping disciples. He said, "It's okay now; it's okay." Then He went to the cross for our sins. What an illustration of perseverance! Luke said He sweat drops of blood He prayed so desperately.

Do you know what it is to weep in prayer? To travail in prayer? Do you know that if you weep for just fifteen minutes, how weak you will become? It's like giving birth to a child.

Jesus rose up after praying and weeping to meet Judas coming with the soldiers. And He went on to Calvary. Jesus persevered, and we must also learn to persevere in prayer. This is not because it's one of the laws of success, but because Jesus told His disciples, "Men ought always to pray and not to faint." Don't be fainthearted. Keep on keeping on. The answer is just around the corner!

Beloved, we can depend upon the faithful, merciful character of our God to answer our prayers when they are for His glory. God looks for opportunities to guarantee His Word to us. So again, don't give up early! A lack of persistent prayer robs God of His pleasure of showing us His "much more" love (Luke 11:13).

Search My Heart, O God...

1. What are the two secrets of the Syrophenician mother who kept persevering in prayer?

    a. _____

    b. _____

2. Consider the roadblocks to the Syrophenician mother's prayer. Am I struggling with any of these roadblocks in my prayer life?

_____

_____

_____

_____

3. Have I overcome any of the roadblocks? How?

_____

_____

_____

_____

4. What is my understanding of God's mercy?

_____

_____

_____

5. In what area of prayer do I need to persevere the most?

_____

_____

_____

_____

Search me, O God, and know my heart: try me, and know my thoughts. (Ps. 139:23)

Chapter 11

THE SECRET TO VICTORY IN
YOUR PRAYER LIFE

I SN'T THERE SOME truth that will help me to be a more victorious, joyous Christian in my prayer life? The answer is yes. And before I tell you the answer, I would like to define what I mean by victory in our prayer life.

Progress from saying a prayer to praying a prayer to becoming a prayer.

My encompassing definition of *victory* means "I'm progressively learning to abide in Christ and His Word. I'm learning to ask what I will and receive answers to my prayers. I have progressed from saying a prayer, to praying a prayer, to becoming a prayer. Yes, my total life becomes a prayer, walking with God. I learn to pray without stopping (1 Thess. 5:17) with a passion to adore and worship God."

Victory means we are growing in faith in the name of Jesus. It is increasing in hearing His voice. Victory also means a determination to be obedient to the Lord. Not only growing in faith but in all His graces that will make a mighty person of prayer. We shall persevere in faith until we see the answers to prayers fulfilled.

Victory is praying from a seated position in Christ with all authority in faith that wrestles Satan to the ground. It is praying with faith and joy that enables one to rest in God's almighty sovereign power, knowing we are the victors in the battle for righteousness (Rom. 14:17).

Above all, victory means prayers are being answered, and God is being glorified in His Son the Lord Jesus Christ. However, my wife reminds me that people usually think of victory as getting what they want. However, victory is what God wants, and there are times when we desperately cry out with Jesus, "If it be possible, remove this cup from me, nevertheless not my will but thine be done."

Rest your soul in these statements of victory:

He must increase, but I must decrease. (John 3:30)

Which is Christ in you, the hope of glory. (Col. 1:27b)

For you died, and your life is hidden with Christ in God. (Col. 3:3)

Victory is ours when we get our focus off our self-effort and on to the gentle Savior's efforts which He is working out for us now in heaven. We must come to appreciate Christ's heavenly work of prayer as much as we appreciate His earthly work on Calvary.

Reliance on Self-Effort

Some Christians seem to be stuck at the point of commitment and are hindered in their prayer lives. They lack freedom, joy, and rest in God because they struggle in relinquishing their self-effort. The secret to victory over fleshly struggles is to know your life is hidden in Christ (Col. 2 and 3). When your life is hidden in Christ, you are not under the law. Remember the law represents self-effort. You are under grace, and herein lies one of the greatest secrets of freedom in one's Christian life. There is a great difference between law and grace.

"Law demands; grace bestows. Law commands but gives no strength to obey. Grace promises and performs, doing everything for us. Law burdens, casts down, and condemns. Grace comforts, strengthens, and makes glad. Law appeals to self to do its utmost; grace points to Christ to do all. Law requires effort and strain, urging us toward a goal we never can reach. Grace works in us all of God's blessed will in us." [17]

The law and self-effort should bring us to a place of utter helplessness.

The spirit of the law is self-effort, and the law of the Old Testament was meant to be a schoolmaster to show us what sin is and the absolute helplessness of our flesh to enable us to obey God. Consequently, the law and self-effort should bring us to a place of utter helplessness. That's good! It's the purpose of the law. And it is at this point where Christians need to know how to have a victorious prayer life.

Jesus Christ's Unfinished Work

We know well what Jesus did on earth for us. We must also come to know well what is doing now in heaven for us. This secret I would call Jesus Christ's unfinished work.

When you first hear this statement about Christ's unfinished work, it may sound like blasphemy. But in truth, there are two aspects to this unfinished work, and they are Jesus Christ's efforts not ours!

First, your prayer life is Christ's unfinished work. Jesus Christ lives today to help you in every respect in your Christian life. We know so well that Jesus's work on the cross saved us. Do you know that Jesus continues to save us? We are Christ's unfinished work.

Second, there is Jesus Christ's unfinished ministry of prayer. His prayer life is still continuing. Hebrews 7:25, 9:24 and Romans 8:34 say that Jesus lives to make intercession for us. His shed blood and ministry of prayer are indispensable in perfecting our Christian character.

The Lord has a great work to do in your life, especially in your prayer life. He wants to use your heart, voice, emotions, and especially your love in prayer. Jesus wants to lead you to trust in God the Father's promises in order to live His life through us. Prayer takes a new dimension when we see this. Prayer is not centered on me, but Christ in me. He uses your unique personality, but prayer becomes Christ in you. Prayer becomes easy, not a drudgery or an impossible task when we discover that Jesus Christ guarantees our victorious prayer life by His victorious prayer life now in heaven for us.

Jesus Christ's work on the cross and work at the right hand of the Father guarantees the new covenant relationship. It is a better covenant!

> This is the covenant that I will make with them after those days, says the Lord: I will put My laws into their hearts, and in their minds I will write them. (Heb. 10:16)

Our salvation is purchased by His blood, and Jesus is a surety, a guarantee for our spiritual life. Therefore, we can find mercy and grace to help in our time of all our needs as we lean upon His grace.

Grace Provides All in Christ

- Do you need forgiveness of sin? He forgives.
- Do you need comfort and strength? He gives comfort and strength.
- Do you need enablement to pray? He gives the enabling grace to pray.
- Do you need victory over temptation? He is there guaranteeing that He will deliver you when you trust and obey Him.
- Do you need more faith? Jesus is the author and finisher of our faith.
- Do you desire to know what to pray? Christ's Holy Spirit will breathe the right prayers through you (Rom. 8:26).

Christ is our life, our entire life, because He is in us and ever lives to pray for us.

God the Father gave a promise and swore an oath that His Son would be a priest forever after the order of Melchizedek, an Old Testament priest and king. He was a type of Jesus Christ, the Coming Eternal King who would offer that one perfect sacrifice and then reign with all authority in the power of the resurrection and endless life. Jesus would be holy, righteous, unblemished, and separate from sinners. He would be a peaceful King, an Eternal King with all heavenly authority behind His name (Heb. 7).

Jesus now appears in the presence of God for us (Heb. 9:24). He is our lawyer priest, shepherd priest, king priest, apostolic priest, captain priest, and brother priest. He is our friend priest and is all in all in order to save us to the uttermost. Yes, He ever lives to make intercession for us. That is His unfinished work until He calls His bride home. He is everything to us. He will be our all-powerful prayer life also if we let Him live His life through our bodies. We are the holy temple of the Holy Spirit. We are to be God's beautiful house of prayer and I refuse to rob God of His good pleasure by not letting Him do His good work in me (Phil. 2:13)!

Paul, the apostle, joyfully cried out in the context of law and grace in Galatians 2:20. His message was this: *Paul is dead. He died on the cross with Jesus Christ. I live here on earth, but not really. Jesus Christ lives in me through His mighty kingly resurrection power.*

The key that brought such mighty power to Paul's life was the key of trusting in the living, resurrected Savior, Jesus Christ, who could now live His life through Paul. Mystery of all mysteries is when Paul continues on, "And the life I now live in the flesh I live by the faith of the Son of God who loved me and gave himself for me" (Gal. 2:20b). Mystery of all mysteries is when we choose to trust in this Almighty Living Son of God who conquered death, and our faith is infused by His faith. His grace strengthens our faith.

You may cry out, "But I don't understand how this works! It seems as though I have so little faith." That may be true. However, you are to take what faith you have and use it. Take your earnest desire, your willing readiness to believe, your firm resolve to obey God, and apply your small mustard seed faith by looking to Jesus. Knowing Him truly as your great Savior and Shepherd, [He wil] l make you complete in every good work to do His will, working in you what is well pleasing in His sight, through Jesus Christ, to whom be glory forever and ever. Amen. (Heb. 13:21)

This verse is especially true of our prayer lives! This is the same principle you use when you apply your faith to obtain the power of electricity. You go over to your light switch and turn it on. Do you understand the power source of the electricity that is coming through hundreds of miles of wires from an electrical atomic plant? You don't really have to understand, but you have enough faith in electrical science to go to the switch and flip it on, expecting the power to come.

This is a picture of how the faith principle works in our Christian lives, and we are instructed, "The just shall live by faith." Faith produces more faith when it is exercised because the grace of our Lord Jesus Christ is always given to those who humbly trust His Word and put their faith in Him, the Great Shepherd of the sheep.

The principle here is that He gives us more grace (James 4:6) and we are changed from glory to glory through Him that lives within us (2 Cor. 3:18).

Andrew Murray writes, "All the feebleness of our Christian life is owing to one thing: we do not know Jesus in heaven; we do not know that Jesus has entered in for us, and that this secures to us boldness and the power of entrance into a heavenly state of life; that He there sits upon the throne as our High Priest, in power, maintaining in us, His own heavenly life; keeping us in personal fellowship with the Living Father, so that in Him we too enter the rest of God. It is because we do not know Jesus in his heavenly life and power that our life is feeble."[18]

The Gentle Character of Our God

Many Christians know and believe what I have been saying. However, they are stuck with only partial truth, and they cannot function in peace. Why? It is because they do not know the gentle character of their God.

Christian teachers and psychologists tell us that Christians are stunted in their Christian growth because they do not know the personality of the God that they love. They see their heavenly Father as a harsh, mean, and demanding father. It is hard for them to relate to Father God as a father of love because they did not have such a relationship here on earth with their fathers. Instead of acceptance and worth, they feel rejection and unworthiness which was heaped upon them by their earthly father. This situation definitely stunts the prayer life of a Christian. Therefore, to understand the secret of prayer life, they need to know and experience their compassionate and gentle Savior.

The secret to power in our prayer lives is knowing the gentle personality of our God.

The Bible says:

> God is love.
> God is spirit.
> God is holy.

I recently counseled a young man who told me, "I don't know who I am. I feel lost and empty inside even though I love Jesus Christ, and I believe the Bible." And he himself admitted, "Though I have an earthly father, I really feel as though I have no father." And this is a problem area with many Christians today. They cannot experience God's fatherly, holy love because of the poor relationship they had with their earthly father.

The secret to power in our prayer lives is knowing the gentle personality of our God to whom we pray. It does no good to believe Christ lives in me and prays for me and is my life unless I know His sweet character. He is not harsh, but He is a God of gentleness and tenderness. David cried out in Psalm 18:35, "Thy gentleness hath made me great" (KJV). In 2 Samuel 22:36, David again says, "Thy gentleness hath made me great" (KJV).

God humbled Himself in great meekness and lowliness to send His Son to die on a cross. Today God continues in His exalted state to humble Himself and bend to our needs to serve us as a shepherd, lawyer, and mediator between God and man. Jesus does this by "ever living to pray for us" and by ministering to us through His Holy Spirit and angels.

In an earlier chapter, I declared that the secret to persevering prayer is to know God as a merciful God. We saw that His mercy is great—it endures forever. It is a manifold mercy, everlasting, and a tender mercy.

I remember an incident that illustrates the opposite of tenderness that has to do with my own earthly father. As a boy, I neglected to cut my fingernails. I recall when my dad would see that they had grown so long he would pull me over to him, sit me down in a chair, and take out his pocket knife to pare my fingernails. He would cut the nails so short that he invariably would draw blood. He was not very tender when it came to cutting my nails and in dealing with me. But our Bible tells us that our Heavenly Father deals with us in tenderness and mercy. His mercy is over all His works.

Tender Mercies over Our Lives

There are five areas that I have found in Scripture where tender mercies are associated with important areas of our lives.

First, in guidance in Psalm 25:6, David cries, "Remember, oh Lord, thy tender mercies and thy lovingkindnesses" (KJV). David had just asked, "Show me Your ways, O Lord, teach me Your paths. Lead me in Your truth and teach me, for You are the God of my salvation; on You I wait all the day." Tender mercies are referred to in relationship to God's ways of leading and teaching us. How comforting this is, in our struggles, to find this is God's will.

Second, tender mercies are referred to in preserving our lives. We know the enemy would try to destroy us in many ways. And so in Psalm 40:11,

David again cries out, "Withhold not thou thy tender mercies from me, O Lord. let thy lovingkindness and thy truth continually preserve me" (KJV). How comforting to feel God's protection in these perilous days.

A third area is when we need forgiveness. Many of us find it hard to receive forgiveness from God or to forgive ourselves. However, God's Word declares He is a God of tender mercies. He desires to deal gently with us in our sin. Psalm 51:1 is a psalm of David's repentance from murder and adultery. He cries, "Have mercy upon me, O God, in your faithful love, in your great tenderness wipe away my offences" (NJB). God could do it because of David's immediate humble repentance. How could anyone not receive such a forgiveness offered in such tenderness to us? This tender forgiveness does not come cheaply. God had to give up His son for us on Calvary!

The fourth important area is in wanting to know God hears our troubled cries. In the great Messianic Psalm 69:16, I believe prophetically it is our Lord speaking in His suffering, "Hear me, oh Lord, for thy loving kindness is good, turn to me according to the multitude of thy tender mercies" (KJV). Sometimes we think God is too busy helping others to hear our needs, but here the psalmist cries, "Hear me in your tender mercies and turn to me according to the multitude of your tender mercies." God will do it. He is a gentle Father, a loving Father.

The fifth important area where we need tenderness is in the area of comfort. A teacher once said to a preaching class, "If you want to be famous and gather great crowds around your preaching, then always speak on comfort." It seems as though we always need to be comforted in one way or another. We read in Psalm 77:9, in the perplexities of problems, David cries out, "Has God forgotten to be gracious? Has He in anger shut up His tender mercies? Selah." In other words, David is saying, "Where are you God? I need your grace; I need your comfort; come and help me."

God's Anger and Mercy

It is interesting that David asks, "Has God's anger overcome His tenderness?" The implied answer is No! It is true that we can anger God when we spurn His love and are constantly rebellious. The rebellious generation of the children of Israel were doomed to die out in the wilderness. However, until they did die, we read that for those forty years God pastured and shepherded these Israelites by the hand of Moses.

Notice in Psalm 77:20, "Thou leddest thy people like a flock by the hand of Moses and Aaron." Psalm 78:52 reads, "But [God] made his own people to go forth like sheep, and guided them in the wilderness like a flock. And He led them on safely, so that they feared not: but the sea overwhelmed their enemies." The point is that in their rebellion God was still a gentle Father, even though at times we see that the wrath of God did come upon the children of disobedience.

He is not a mean God.

We are warned in Colossians 3:5- 6 not to practice sin or else the wrath of God can come upon us. Yet, God remembers mercy in His anger, and He always chastises us for our good. In the end, He is not a mean God; He is always a God of love, a God of kindness and ready to show tender mercies and gentleness to all who turn to Him with a humble heart. The classic illustration of this is the story of the prodigal son in Luke 15.

God's Gentleness in the New Testament

The following are some more beautiful illustrations in the New Testament of how Jesus, Paul, Peter, and John exemplified these shepherding and nurse-maid principles of tender mercies to the childish, unbelieving, and even rebellious disciples.

On Jesus's last night, when He washed the feet of the unbelieving and squabbling disciples, He addressed them with the tender words "little children" in John 13:33. You and I would have been upset by their unbelief. But not Jesus. He says, "Little children, I'm only going to be with you a little while longer." How beautiful.

After our Lord's crucifixion and resurrection, He appeared several times to His disciples. The Lord dealt gently with "Doubting Thomas," who was honest enough to express his true feelings.

All the disciples were in unbelief for a while. In the Sea of Galilee, they had gone fishing after His resurrection, and they didn't know what to do. Peter had denied his Lord. In fact, they had all denied Him. What would Jesus say? What would He do when He saw them again?

Well, Jesus prepared a breakfast for them and looked out to their boat and called unto them. He was not harsh and mean, but, again, He said, "Lads, do you have any meat to eat?" (*Lads* is a tender word, a friendly word.) Oh, how tender our Lord was with His denying, unbelieving disciples. Jesus proceeded to heal Peter's heart and reassure him of His love.

The aged apostle John learned well from his master as he declared tenderly to Christians sixty years later, "My little children, I write these things unto you, so that you may sin not" (1 John 2:1a). He wrote to the older fathers, he wrote to the young men who were overcomers, and then he writes to the little children: "I write to you, little children, because you have known the Father" (1 John 2:13).

History says of aged John that he had come to have only one sermon: "brethren, love one another." The apostle Paul's statement shows again this whole concept of God's tender mercies toward us most beautifully in 1 Thessalonians 2:7 when he writes, "But we were gentle among you, just as a nursing mother cherishes her own children." That's how Paul dealt with the Church. That's how God, the Father, deals with us.

Beloved, the fruit of the Holy Spirit is love, joy, peace, longsuffering, gentleness, goodness, faith, meekness, and self-control. The Holy Spirit is a spirit of gentleness with us all throughout our Christian lives. If there is any pain of harshness, it is not from God to us, but it is from us to God, causing Him pain. God had pain when He sent His Son to die for us. God somehow has pain when He births us.

Paul says in Galatians 4:19, "My little children, of whom I travail in birth…" (KJV). God travailed in birth through Paul to win the Galatians to Christ. But He says, "I travail in birth again until Christ be formed in you." And so God is the greatest sufferer in this universe. God is love, and love always suffers. "Love suffers long and is kind" (1 Cor. 13:4).

Summary

Beloved, the secret of a successful prayer life is to know that we rest in grace. We rest in the risen Christ whose work is not finished. He ever lives to pray for us. He lives to be our mediator between God and man. He lives to be our intercessor. He lives to help us grow up, and He shepherds us. Jesus Christ is our all in all.

We look to Him for His strength, His grace, and His mercy for all we need in our Christian lives. Also, remember that this secret to a fuller prayer life includes knowing that God the Father's personality is like unto that of a mother nursing her child to maturity. God is a gentle Father full of tender mercies to His own. Learn today with David, "Your gentleness has made me great" (Ps. 18:35). And this gentleness will make you a great Christian also in your prayer life as you yield yourself fully to your living Savior, who is perfecting your prayer life through the power of the Holy Spirit.

Search My Heart, O God...

1. Do I see God the Father as gentle and merciful toward me? _____

2. What are some of the aspects of the character of God that I enjoy the most?

_____

_____

_____

_____

3. What is the secret to victory in my prayer life?

_____

_____

_____

_____

Search me, O God, and know my heart: try me, and know my thoughts. (Ps. 139:23)

Chapter 12

A SECRET TO GREATER FAITH: PRAYER AND FASTING

THERE IS ANOTHER secret we must enter into in order to have power in prayer: fasting. Fasting gives spiritual victory when nothing else avails. When all else fails, fall into the arms of Jesus with prayer and fasting. Has God begun to deal with you yet on this subject of fasting? I began thinking about this subject over twenty-five years ago when I was a pastor in a Baptist church in Gladwin, Michigan.

I recall speaking to an evangelist friend about this subject, and he shocked me with this statement: "Oh, that must be for the Old Testament. You never hear any of the great leaders of today speak about fasting. It's not spoken about at all in our Bible conferences." He was right about the lack of teaching on the matter at the time. Within the last decade, prayer has begun to come back into the Church and so has this great biblical truth of fasting.

Our Lord Jesus calls victorious Christians "overcomers" as He speaks to the seven churches in the book of Revelation. Jesus has many rewards for those who overcome the world, the flesh, and the devil. We can be overcoming Christians. We should be because the Lord has paid the price for us to be overcomers.

Bible Basis for Fasting

Fasting appears at least sixty times in the Bible. Fasting appears thirty-two times in the Old Testament, and I have counted at least twenty-eight times in the New Testament. Some of these times refer to the wrong type of fasts, such as people who engage in religious fasts with much pride and much pomp and ceremony to show off their religiosity. This does not negate the fact that this is a special spiritual exercise that we are to follow.

Fasting is so special that today even Satan is imitating it with his followers in the satanic worship movement. Thousands of witches and their followers are practicing fasting on a weekly basis, praying to Satan to send out his forces to overthrow Christian evangelists and to wreck Christian pastors' homes and marriages. I do not give Satan primary recognition for the fall of many of our great public evangelists, nor do I give him much recognition for the multitude of Christian homes and pastors' homes that have been wrecked by sin and divorce. The Word of God says what we sow, we will reap (Gal. 6:7). God's Word says, "Be sure your sin will find you out" (Num. 32:23).

The ministers of the gospel—apostles, prophets, pastors, evangelists, and teachers—all have an awesome responsibility to call the Church back to prayer and fasting in these days of decline and sin. I believe it will be an awesome yet sad day at the judgment seat of Christ when we shall all be judged according to our works, whether good or bad.

> "Now, therefore," says the Lord, "turn to Me with all your heart, with fasting, with weeping, and with mourning." So rend your heart, and not your garments; return to the Lord your God, for He is gracious and merciful, slow to anger, and of great kindness; and He relents from doing harm…Blow the trumpet in Zion, consecrate a fast, call a solemn assembly; gather the people, sanctify the congregation, assemble the elders, gather the children and nursing babes; let the bridegroom go out from his chamber, and the bride from her dressing room. Let the priests, who minister to the Lord, weep between the porch and the altar; let them say, "Spare Your people, O Lord, and do give not Your heritage to reproach, that the nations should rule over them. Why should they say among the peoples, 'Where is their God?'" (Joel 2:12-13, 15-17)

This call to prayer and fasting and weeping before the Lord came in a day of spiritual decline in Israel. The northern kingdom had already gone into captivity many years past, and the prophets were saying that Judah would also follow them into judgment. But Judah would not listen, and they too became sinful and disobedient to the Word of God. In this context comes the call for fasting and prayer.

Has God ever called you to a time of prayer and fasting? In the Bible, great men and women of all ages practiced fasting: Moses, David, Esther, Ezra, Nehemiah, Isaiah, Daniel, Jesus, Paul, the apostles, and the leaders of the early Church.

Jesus said that when we fast, we should not make an open show of it (Matt. 6:16-18). He did not say "if" but "when." He also said, "But the days will come when the bridegroom will be taken away from them, and then they will fast in those days" (Mark 2:20).

Two Powerful Purposes for Fasting

Beloved, fasting will do two wonderful basic things for your spiritual life. First, you will experience power in prayer. Second, fasting will draw you nearer to the heart of God to experience His loving presence and intimacy more than you ever have before. This will result in increased faith to take hold of the promises of God.

Fasting is not primarily to harness God's power but to harness our flesh.

This is true because one of the great purposes of fasting is not primarily to change God's mind about some answer to petition, but to change our minds. Fasting is not primarily to harness God's power but to harness our flesh. Fasting is desperately needed to rearrange our priorities and our appetites. These appetites normally follow in this sequence:

Food

Sex

Materialism

Hunger for spiritual realities

How can our prayers be really effective if we are in bondage to our flesh?

Jesus said, "Seek first the kingdom of God" (Matt. 6:33). We are to love the

Lord our God with all our heart, mind, soul, and strength. That is the First Commandment. After fasting with prayer and reading the Word of God, our priorities for food, sex, and materialism become rearranged, and a spiritual desire for God becomes first.

How can our prayers be really effective if we are in bondage to our flesh with overindulgence in food, fun, and fleshly pleasures?

> All things are lawful for me, but not all things are helpful; all things are lawful for me, but not all things edify. (1 Cor. 10:23)

> And every man that striveth for the mastery is temperate in all things. Now they do it to obtain a corruptible crown; but we an incorruptible. I therefore so run, not as uncertainly; so fight I, not as one that beatest the air: but I keep under my body, and bring it into subjection: lest that by any means, when I have preached to others, I myself should be a castaway. (1 Cor. 9:25-26)

Jesus warns in Luke 21:34, with a view toward His second coming:

> "Be on guard so that your hearts are not weighed down with dissipation and drunkenness and the worries of life, and that day does not catch you unexpectedly, like a trap. For it will come upon all who live on the face of the whole earth. Be alert at all times, praying that you may have the strength to escape all these things that will take place, and to stand before the Son of Man." (RSV)

How can we say, "Jesus is Lord," if we have other powers over us which we cannot break, such as uncontrolled appetites for food, materialism, and sex? We must have Jesus's power. We must be in control of our lives by the power of the Holy Spirit.

The Holy Spirit wants to lead us to that place of experiencing the power of God in our lives where Jesus truly is Lord, the master over our appetites, where Jesus controls our finances, homes, businesses, and families. Christians must first experience God's power within before they can be mighty in prayer to experience God's power pouring out.

It has been said that Jesus is not Lord at all unless He *is* Lord of all. Jesus can only be Lord when He is Lord of *all*. It is a shame that so many Christians are digging their own graves with their knives and forks. It is a shame that the advertisements of the world, the allurement of the world system, have so caused them to spend to "keep up with the Joneses."

It is an absolute travesty to hear of so many young, unmarried Christians conceiving children out of the covenant of marriage, as well as the number of Christian marriages failing because of the sin of adultery. Where is the power of God? Where is the God of Israel? Where is this powerful, resurrected Jesus Christ in the life of the Christian Church?

Yes, Jesus is there, and He is real. We simply are not using His Lordship power to overcome. We are not choosing for Him to be Lord at the moments of temptation. We can be overcomers. The Church can be a glorious bride, a beautiful bride without spot or wrinkle if we will adhere to the spiritual discipline of prayer, fasting, and seeking the Lord with all our hearts.

Fasting is an act that humbles us.

The second great secret of fasting is that fasting humbles a Christian: body, soul, and spirit. The key verse for revival seems to be in 2 Chronicles 7:14.

If My people who are called by My name will humble themselves, and pray and seek My face, and turn from their wicked ways, then I will hear from heaven, and will forgive their sin and heal their land.

Have you ever noticed what the first thing is in that list in order to get revival? It takes the humbling of ourselves and praying and earnest seeking of God's face before we can even repent. For the next thing is to turn from our wicked ways. Fasting is an act that humbles us and empowers us to overcome.

Christians Don't Have to Sin

By their lives, many Christians are saying, "I love sin too much. I love the world too much. I love the way I'm living more than I love the Christian way in which I should walk." Then they wonder why they cannot break this power over them. The answer is failing to humble themselves in fasting and prayer.

A wonderful young Christian man had a terrible spirit of jealousy in his marriage. He couldn't help himself. He went into rages of jealousy. I believe this was his second marriage. He had become a Christian, and he wanted to save his marriage. He didn't know what to do. He was advised to go into three days of fasting and prayer.

I will never forget the radiance from this brother's life when God showed him the root cause of his jealousy. He was angry at his mother who had betrayed his father's love, and he had harbored this anger almost subconsciously. He then in turn took his anger out against his wife. When God showed that to him, he began to be set free, and God gave him grace to forgive his mother. I will never forget how happy he was and how victorious he was after those three days of prayer and fasting.

Christians are going to counselors and psychologists with the problems of their innermost beings and trying to get answers. Most counselors are not telling them that some of the answer is in humbling themselves before God with fasting and prayer. The tentacles of sin go so deep in our lives, and habits are easily formed.

I remember a young, handsome man who cried out in despair to his pastor, "I cannot think a pure thought." He sounded like the apostle Paul who said, "O wretched man that I am! Who will deliver me from this body of death?" (Rom. 7:24). Paul then writes to the Corinthians, "But we had the sentence of death in ourselves, that we should not trust in ourselves, but in God which raiseth the dead: who delivered us from so great a death, and doth deliver: in whom we trust that He will yet deliver us" (2 Cor. 1:9-10 KJV).

Yes, Jesus Christ will deliver us if we let Him. Fasting humbles us as we let go of food and materialism, and as we let go of our flesh, we shut ourselves up with God in prayer to seek Him and Him alone.

I believe the New Testament scripture for revival is James chapter four, and it is rarely quoted as much as 2 Chronicles 7:14. However, in this chapter, after the questions of why are there wars and fighting among you, the answer is their inner lusts and envious desires. It is interesting that God says what you really want you don't have because you ask not and receive not. And if you do ask, you ask amiss so that it may be consumed on your lusts.

Some of the strongest words against Christians in the New Testament are used where James rebuked the Christians in his circle.

> Adulterers and adulteresses! Do you not know that friendship with the world is enmity with God? ...But He gives more grace. Therefore He says: "God resists the proud, but gives grace to the humble." Therefore

submit to God. Resist the devil and he will flee from you. (James 4:4, 6-7).

The first rule of success in the kingdom of God is given by Jesus in the Sermon on the Mount when He said, "Blessed are the poor in spirit, for theirs is the kingdom of heaven" (Matt. 5:3). The one indispensable condition of true fellowship with Jesus is humility. All other graces flow forth from the root of humbling ourselves before God. David cries out in Psalm 35:13, "But as for me, when they were sick, my clothing was sackcloth; I humbled myself with fasting."

Also the messianic Psalm 69:10-11 (AMP) reads, "When I wept and humbled myself with fasting, I was jeered at and humiliated. When I made sackcloth my clothing, I became a byword (an object of scorn) to them." This is no doubt referring not only to David but to Jesus Christ who fasted for forty days and nights before He began His public ministry. Good, religious people often do not understand about fasting and will speak against it, but I emphatically declare to you that the main reason for practicing prayer with fasting is that the Word of God teaches it. And we must obey the Word of God and not regard what man says.

My friend, I have now shared with you the two great, powerful purposes for fasting.

First, we fast to rearrange our priorities in order to put God first in our lives.

Second, we fast for the power to humble ourselves to be broken and empty of self before God.

It is a voluntary humbling on our part to put away certain things. There are other events that will humble our souls in life—sickness, accident, death, wars. But how much better it is when we humble ourselves.

More Startling Results

There are other startling results to fasting mentioned in Scripture. For instance, fasting with repentance averted God's judgment on Nineveh. Also, seeking the Lord with fasting can give special wisdom and understanding of God's plan and Word. Daniel found this to be so in Daniel 9:2-3 and 9:21. Fasting also helps set the captive free (Isa. 58:6).

Jesus said the demon-possessed child could not be set free "by anything but prayer and fasting" in Mark 9:29. Truly prayer and fasting intensify our prayers. Faith grows as we let go of earthly things and take hold of the Father. We claim the Father's prayer promises with new faith and thus great mountains are moved.

Combined Fasting and Prayer Overcomes Lust

I want to personally attest again to the power of prayer and fasting to break the power of sin and temptation. Earlier I told you how a day and night of prayer and fasting broke a satanic temptation over me for a woman. Now I want to tell you about another temptation that I believe was due more to my own lust. These inward temptations are much harder to break I feel than the temptations that come from without.

I had led a lovely lady to Christ, and as I was trying to disciple her, I found myself becoming attracted to her very quickly. I thought, "Am I falling in love with her?" I could tell she felt the same attraction. We came to the point where we admitted it. I knew that as a married man some twenty-five to thirty years, I had a problem. It is no sin to have temptations. I believe it is very important for Christians to realize this. There are several stages to temptation, according to James 1:14-15:

> Enticement,
>
> Allurement,
>
> Accepting the temptation,
>
> Willingly falling into sin.

I was being tempted, enticed, and allured. Would I permit temptation to be birthed into sin?

Now, the first thing I did was tell my wife. That's right! Because I knew she was an understanding woman, and I knew she would pray for me. I believe she also knew that I would fight this thing, and I did. I went on a week's Daniel fast. I had an assignment at a youth camp to teach, but there I could still practice the Daniel fast as described in Daniel 10:3. No delicacies, nor meat, nor wine entered my mouth for three whole weeks.

As I practiced this at youth camp, I ate only some small portions and no desserts. Some meals were skipped entirely and the time was spent in prayer.

When I returned home, I found this experience extremely valuable and effective, so I continued to push away food from my mouth and cry out from my heart to God constantly for victory. The temptation was snapped, broken by the power of the name of the Lord Jesus Christ, and victory was mine. Jesus said to Peter, "I have prayed for you, that your faith should not fail" (Luke 22:32). And I could hear Jesus saying to me, "Leon, I have prayed for you that you fail not." The combination of fasting and prayer works.

There is no reason for Christians to fall into sin.

> No temptation has overtaken you except such as is common to man; but God is faithful, who will not allow you to be tempted beyond what you are able, but with the temptation will also make the way of escape, that you may be able to bear it. (1 Cor. 10:13)

We are responsible for sinning. God will help us not to practice sin if we purpose in our hearts to keep our hearts pure by clinging to Him through prayer and fasting.

It is so wonderful to experience communion with Almighty God, our Lord Jesus Christ. The apostle Paul writes, in essence, "I count everything lost. I've counted everything as refuse for the excellency of the knowledge of Christ Jesus my Lord. That I might know Him and the power of His resurrection and the fellowship of His suffering. That I might experience a practical resurrection from the dead, that I can say, it is not I that lives but Christ lives in me" (Phil. 3:8-11, paraphrased).

Paul says, "Not that I have already attained, or am already perfected; but I press on, that I may lay hold of that for which Christ Jesus has also laid hold of me" (Phil. 3:12).

It is truly life; it is bread. Jesus understood. He said, "I have food to eat of which you do not know...My food is to do the will of Him who sent Me, and to finish His work" (John 4:32,34).

To be drawn to God is the water of life. Paul wanted to apprehend that for which he was apprehended. This is having communion with God as Adam walked with God in the Garden of Eden. He enjoyed God, His Creator's presence, His guidance and comfort. With His help and power to do His will, this is indeed abundant life.

Jesus's Secret of Victory

When we look at our Savior's life, this was what He desired: to do the Father's will and to walk with His Father. Their relationship could truly be described as intimate communion. We have a very beautiful verse in Psalm 22: 19–20 which describes a close-up look at Jesus on the cross, showing His intense love and communion with the Father. In verse twenty we read of His sufferings, "Deliver Me from the sword, (My darling) My precious life from the power of the dog." (KJV)

The phrase *my darling* is literally translated "my only one," and in Christ's sufferings He cried out, "My darling, my only one, my only life, deliver me from the dog (from execution agent)." Obviously the scholars of that day chose to put forth the close relationship of Jesus with the Father, instead of translating *my darling, my only one* as referring to Christ's only precious life.

I believe "my darling" is a good translation, as Jesus earlier said that God was His Lord, His strength. And on the cross He cried, "Father, Father." God created us to walk with Him and enjoy His presence. God desires our love and communion. In Jeremiah 31:3, in regards to Israel we read, "Yes, I have loved you with an everlasting love; therefore with lovingkindness I have drawn you." In the book of Hosea in Chapter 11:4 God speaks of the adulterous nation, Israel, but He cries, "I drew them with gentle cords, with bands of love..."

In the Song of Solomon 1:4 the bridegroom of the bride says, "Draw me away! We will run after you." This is the highest joy of life, to be drawn by God by the power of His Holy Spirit in sweet communion, and we receive this through the benefit of prayer and fasting.

Secret Fasting is Necessary

I remind you that Jesus's first lesson on prayer was to tell us, "But you, when you pray, go into your room, and when you have shut your door, pray to your Father who is in the secret place; and your Father who sees in secret will reward you openly" (Matt. 6:6). The chamber is a place of retirement, of privacy, of intimacy. Our highest joy with the Father comes from being in this chamber with Him.

The practice of secret prayer with fasting leads to the practice of great corporate praying. Our leaders need to make their churches houses of prayer to teach the lambs and sheep this great truth to go and be alone with the

Father. It is truly one of the greatest needs of every Christian's life, and lack of prayer is the basis for the failure of the Church to be empowered to do its job to go into all the world and preach the gospel in the power of the living Jesus Christ.

Fasting with prayer is necessary for growth in our Christian journeys. We will grow in faith because our spirits will grow in the blessedness of "poorness." We will grow in faith that moves mountains because we have let our Lord move our false priorities.

We will have new power in prayer because we are learning to walk in new dimensions of His presence. Fasting truly helps us say, "He must increase, but I must decrease" (John 3:30). The man who said this was John the Baptist, who lived very simply on locust and honey. He understood fasting, and, according to Christ, He understood Jesus's identity more than anyone else.

Search My Heart, O God...

1. Consider the strongest appetites within the soul of every human being—food, sex, materialism, and hunger for spiritual realities. Is there one area in which you've been praying for victory? _____ Take a moment now and ask the Lord to lead you into a fast that will strengthen you and enable you to overcome in this area of strongest temptation.

2. Study and possibly highlight key verses from Matthew 4:1-11 and Acts 13:1-4 in your Bible. What appetite did Satan appeal to in Jesus the first time he tempted Him?

_____

3. What appetite did Satan first appeal to in the Garden of Eden when he tempted Eve?

_____

4. Note that the Christians in Acts 13:1-4 fasted and ministered to the Lord regarding the appointment of leadership. How can this type of prayer apply to my life?

_____

_____

_____

_____

How could this type of fast possibly apply to the house of prayer that I might be called to lead?

_____

_____

_____

_____

5. What does it mean to me to minister to the Lord?

_____

_____

_____

_____

*Search me, O God, and know my heart: try
me, and know my thoughts. (Ps. 139:23)*

Conclusion

A PERSONAL WORD TO YOU FROM THE AUTHOR, LEON FRANCK

M Y FRIEND, YOU are special to me because I believe you have a heart to pray—so much so that you took the time to read this book on building a house of prayer! Thank you for reading my book.

God has a special plan for your life, and I would like to encourage you to remember that our Great Shepherd, Jesus Christ, calls each sheep by name and walks ahead of them and leads them forward into a place of promise and reward.

> ...[A]nd the sheep hear his voice: and he calleth his own sheep by name, and leadeth them out. And when he putteth forth his own sheep, he goeth before them, and the sheep follow him: for they know his voice. (John 10:3-4)

In closing, I hope to encourage you further in your personal prayer life by sharing briefly how our Great Shepherd fulfilled a few of my dreams and led me into a rich land of promise and reward. If Jesus did this for me, He will surely lead you in your dreams as well.

One of my **first** dreams was centered on EVANGELISM coupled with prayer. I enjoyed my work as a pastor for nine years, but I had a burning desire to get out of that little church and reach our tri-state area—Iowa, Minnesota, and Wisconsin—for Christ. I resigned the church and told the Lord that if I was going to truly do a work for Him, I'd need a secretary.

One of our first goals was to start a coffee house as a youth center. I set up a prayer meeting with eight other pastors to pray over this outreach. A woman who I had never met before walked into the prayer meeting.

Afterward, I walked her to the car and she said, "God wants me to be your secretary."

I was thrilled! I asked her, "How much will you need to live on?"

She considered this and told me she could live on $158.00 a month!

She was hired! Unbelievably, this woman was a secretary in a government office—and God sent her to us!

For six years, Arlene and I joined hands and hearts to hold rallies and prayer meetings. We had decision cards at the rallies, and I was thrilled to count five thousand decisions for Christ through our tri-state outreaches. God is good!

One person who knew my ministry from those years greeted me the other day in a restaurant, and when he introduced me to his friends he said, "This is the Billy Graham of LaCrosse." I certainly never thought of it that way, but I felt encouraged by his words.

My **second** dream was one of my greatest dreams, to write a BOOK ON PRAYER. Again, I prayed, "God, I need a secretary. I don't know how to do this."

I was in a prayer meeting in a large retreat center in Florida when a single mother with a ten-year-old daughter approached me and said, "I want to move to Wisconsin, and I'll write your book." Arlene and I lived at Prayer Valley at the time and so this young mother sold her home and her earthly goods and moved to Wisconsin with her daughter. She stayed for a year and a half and helped me to write my book.

The book you're holding in your hands right now is the second edition of that book.

The **third** dream that I had was a strong desire to SUPPORT MY FAMILY. Because I grew up poor and orphaned as a child, I didn't want my family to experience that kind of poverty. As a pastor and prayer minister, I had no Social Security, no pension plans, and no retirement plan.

Unbelievably, a man who was a pastor from Iowa traveled a long distance to tell me how he was going to take care of his six kids and support his family by remodeling and then selling old homes and apartments. He wanted to help me do the same for my family. It clicked! I knew I was to follow his lead and also buy an apartment to remodel, repair, and resell in my spare time. As a family we did it. We ended up with several apartments which covered our living expenses and our future retirement—and we became self-supporting. My wife and children helped to clean, paint, and refurbish the apartments. Later, my son and his wife took it over and managed it.

This financial liberty enabled me to fulfill my **fourth** dream—to travel the United States and SEE THE KINGDOM OF GOD. I traveled on and off for ten years with Ray Bringham, a man who had a vision to start Prayer Summits. We had the first Washington, D.C. Prayer Summit, and God blessed our gatherings mightily.

There's more! Probably my greatest dream was to have a PRAYER RETREAT CENTER with a school. Of course, I believe God placed this dream in my heart, and it was actually our dream together. I prayed and asked God to give us the property. It took ten years of waiting on the Lord before the property finally came into our hands. In the end, we traded our own house as a down payment and purchased a 186-acre farm in a beautiful valley with a barn, swimming pool, tennis court, and thirty-two-room lodge! God has used Prayer Valley to build a great house of prayer that shines to the heavens even today.

As you can see, God is good! Arlene and I will soon enter our eighties, and I can testify that in all our years together the Lord Jesus has been our Good Shepherd, always going before us to lead us through many trials and tests and into our land of promises come true.

My friend, seek the Lord Jesus with all of your heart about your dreams and pray with faith. While you lead His sheep to build a house of prayer, remember that He is ever leading you into your land of promises come true.

> "For I know the plans I have for you," declares the LORD, "plans to prosper you and not to harm you, plans to give you hope and a future. Then you will call upon me and come and pray to me, and I will listen to you" (Jer. 29:11-12)

"I shall be anointed with fresh oil"

—Psalm 92:10b

PRAYER PRINCIPLES AT A GLANCE

FOR THOSE TIMES when you are in a hurry and need a quick reference, I want to leave you with a brief summary of the prayer principles shared throughout this book:

1. Appoint a leader to be responsible to start the meeting, engage prayers, and conclude the meeting at the announced time.

2. All persons should feel welcome and as special as the Lord has created them to be (1 Cor. 12).

3. Make prayers aware of the progression of the meeting:
     a. Anticipation of God's blessings and answers.
     b. Adoration of Him who is the Lamb of God who takes away the sin of the world.
     c. Participation of each member to create a symphony of praise and petition to the glory of God.
     d. Exhilaration of our spirits as we obey and pray to Him who said, "For My house shall be called a house of prayer for all nations" (Isa. 56:7). Remember, "Ask, and you will receive, that your joy may be full" (John 16).

4. Encourage all to have a Bible present and to learn to pray the promises of God (Heb. 4:12 and John 15:7).

5. It is ideal to minister to the Lord in song by having a musician present to start a psalm, hymn, or spiritual song (Col. 3:16). Everyone should feel free at the Holy Spirit's prompting to start a chorus or song. Music brings down the presence of God. The psalmist says over ninety times, "Sing unto the Lord."

6. Encourage all to pray before coming to the meeting and to have daily private prayers at home in secret (Matt. 6:6).

7. A small prayer group is fine. Jesus had a group of twelve to disciple. Ideally, a large prayer meeting will be made up of many small ones.

8. It is fine to heal the prayer warriors who are in attendance before you pray for other requests (James 5:16).

9. It only takes twenty seconds to say the Lord's Prayer. Jesus's prayers were short; therefore, try to keep your prayers brief, and let everyone pray several times as the Spirit leads.

10. Keep exalting the Lord Jesus Christ in all your prayers by quoting His words and prayer promises and by remembering He is praying with you and through you as our great High Priest (Heb. 4:14-16).

11. Do not fear silence, but treasure times of being still and knowing He is God (Ps. 46:10).

12. Learn to focus by listening to the Holy Spirit. He will guide and teach us when to merge in prayer, when to be still, and when to share in scripture, poem, psalm, etc.

13. No prayer meetings are alike. The Holy Spirit's flow is different in every meeting, so expect prayer meetings to become more glorious.

14. Endeavor to aim for "laser-beam focus praying." It is all right to have several different people pray for the same thing. Others bring forth different scriptures, intensities, and even tears. Faith and assurance build as prayer increases.

15. Go with His flow. The leader can sense by the Holy Spirit when the group should change direction to proceed to another subject.

16. Prayer meetings are worthy of our best efforts in planning for attendance, participation, inspiration, and comfort.

17. Comfort? Be aware of physical infirmities of those present, especially back or leg problems. A hard, straight-back arm chair works best for most back problems. For longer prayer meetings, a recliner is best for serious back problems.

18. Attempt to build a sense of unity and one accord from the beginning to the end of the meeting. First, ask the Holy Spirit to do

it. Then read out loud together scripture verses such as Matthew 18:19. Through scripture promises, praises, and adoration, unity builds. Also, verbal agreement (such as saying, "Amen") with others builds unity.

19. Encourage all to come to the prayer meetings. Help the timid and fearful by welcoming them and giving them a scripture promise verse to read out loud in the meetings. Find easy ways for them to participate. Most people know the Lord's Prayer, and praying this out loud together is a great ice breaker and starting point.

20. Each person's voice is unique and special to God. Teach that each person is important and that God wants to hear his or her voice in prayer to be part of God's special prayer symphony. It is okay to start a meeting will all people praying and praising the Lord out loud together; ten to fifteen minutes. This unashamed praying and praising the Lord brings down the Holy Spirit.

ENDNOTES

CHAPTER 1

1. John Peter Lange, *Lange's Commentary of the Holy Scriptures*, Book of Isaiah, ed. Philip Schaff (Grand Rapids, MI: Zondervan Publishing House), 607.

2. Justification is expounded from Romans 3:21 through to the end of Chapter 5, and Galatians 3 and 4. There are some scattered verses in other epistles of both doctrines. However, Hebrews Chapters 1-10 is primarily all about Christ's exalted priesthood. You might be surprised if you compare the total number of verses of each doctrine.

CHAPTER 2

3. John Franklin, *A House Of Prayer* (Nashville, TN: LifeWay Press, 2002).

4. Stormie Omartian, *The Power of a Praying® Husband* and *The Power of a Praying® Wife* (Eugene, OR: Harvest House Publishers, 2001 and 2007, respectively).

5. Franklin.

6. Cheryl Sacks, *The Prayer-Saturated Church* (Colorado Springs, CO: NavPress, 2007).

7. Daniel Henderson with Margaret Saylar, *Fresh Encounters: Experiencing Transformation through United Worship-Based Prayer* (Colorado Springs, CO: NavPress, 2008).

CHAPTER 3

8. George Verver, (lecture, Campus Crusade Missionary Conference, University of Illinois, Urbana, IL, 1993).

CHAPTER 5

9. Armin Gesswein, *With One Accord in One Place* (Camp Hill, PA: Christian Publications, 1978), 13-15.

10. *The New York Courier*, 1980.

11. Ibid.

CHAPTER 6

12. *Vine's Expository Dictionary of New Testament Words* (Nashville, TN: Royal Publishers, Inc., 1952).

CHAPTER 7

13. Evelyn Christensen and Viola Blake, *What Happens When Women Pray* (Colorado Springs, CO: Cook Communications Ministries, 1992).

14. Statistics from http://www.worldmission.cc/.

CHAPTER 10

15. Karl Barth, *Church Dogmatics*, vol.1, *Doctrine of God* (London: T. & T. Clark Ltd; new edition, 2009), 411.

16. Wesley L. Duewel, *Mighty Prevailing Prayer* (Grand Rapids, MI: Zondervan Publishing House, 1990) 87-88.

CHAPTER 11

17. Andrew Murray, *The Ministry of Intercession* (New Kensignton, PA: Whitaker House, 1982), 60.

18. Andrew Murray, *The Holiest of All* (Ada, MI: Fleming H. Revell Publishing Company, 1934), 149.

IF YOU'RE A FAN OF THIS BOOK, PLEASE TELL OTHERS...

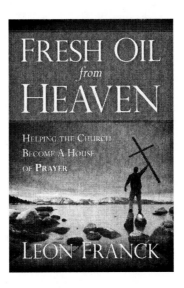

- Write about *Fresh Oil From Heaven—Helping the Church Become a House of Prayer* on your blog, Twitter, MySpace, and Facebook page.
- Suggest *Fresh Oil From Heaven—Helping the Church Become a House of Prayer* to friends.
- When you're in a bookstore, ask them if they carry the book. The book is available through all major distributors, so any bookstore that does not have *Fresh Oil From Heaven— Helping the Church Become a House of Prayer* in stock can easily order it.
- Write a positive review of *Fresh Oil From Heaven—Helping the Church Become a House of Prayer* on www.amazon.com.
- Send my publisher, HigherLife Publishing, suggestions on Web sites, conferences, and events you know of where this book could be offered at media@ahigherlife.com.
- Purchase additional copies to give away as gifts.

CONNECT WITH ME...

To learn more about *Fresh Oil From Heaven—Helping the Church Become a House of Prayer*, if you would like someone to pray with you, or perhaps talk about building a house of prayer, feel free to contact me.

Rev. Leon Franck
710 Krueger Court
Onalaska, Wisconsin 54650
Phone: (608) 783 - 7727
Email: lafranck@aol.com

You may also contact my publisher directly:

HigherLife Publishing
400 Fontana Circle
Building 1 – Suite 105
Oviedo, Florida 32765
Phone: (407) 563-4806
Email: media@ahigherlife.com

And God bless you as you help build a house of prayer for His people!